Broken and Transformed

ISBN: 1-4791-4585-8
ISBN-13: 9781479145850

Broken and Transformed

Moving beyond life's difficult times

Kristi Lemley

2012

Dedication

This book is dedicated to many people. I first and foremost want to thank my husband, Kraig. Your love, support, and encouragement have meant so much to me. I look forward to the years ahead. To my Mom, Dad and June, Kari, Kelli, Ron, and Christie and the rest of my family and friends you have always been there for me and I would not be where I am today without you. To Mom and Nancy thank you for your initial editing. To Nancy, Ken, and Kraig thank you for opening up your life story in order to help others. To the prayer team- words cannot describe the appreciation I have for your unending prayers; you have helped me hold my arms up. To the women in the i-connect ministry group thank you for your support, feedback, and continued focus to keep going.

I thank each one of you for helping me on this journey. I pray God blesses each one of you because you have richly blessed my life.

TABLE OF CONTENTS

SECTION ONE   PAGE

Chapter 1   Broken by a Past—My Story (My Ministry)   3

Chapter 2   Broken by Divorce—Nancy's Story   9

Chapter 3   Broken by Cancer—Ken's Story   15

Chapter 4   Broken by Life Changes—Kraig's Story   21

Chapter 5   Broken by Ministry—My Story   27

SECTION TWO

Chapter 6   A Place Called Broken   37

Chapter 7   Finding Peace with God   45

Chapter 8   God Will Fight for You   53

Chapter 9   Identifying with Christ   57

Chapter 10   Christ Your Savior   63

Chapter 11   Life in the Word   69

Chapter 12   Forgiveness   79

Chapter 13   Battleground   89

Chapter 14   Take off Your Grave Cloths   103

Chapter 15   The Exchange   117

CONCLUSION

Chapter 16   Refreshing Times   129

APPENDIX A   Scriptures Utilized   135

APPENDIX B   References   139

LETTER FROM KRISTI   140

~ INTRODUCTION ~

When I was younger and very active in sports, I would hear my coaches say, "No pain, no gain." I always rolled my eyes and I have to admit, my thoughts toward them were not positive. However, as the season would progress, I found it was true. When I worked and pushed myself physically then I would become stronger, faster, and better able to do whatever sport I was in at the time. I find that I am encouraging myself with these same words as I exercise today.

What does this have to do with being broken? In my mind, everything! Let me explain. When everything seems to be going well in life, you go about your daily routine without much thought. How deep does your relationship with God grow when everything is good—honestly? Do you constantly call out to God and hold on to Him with every fiber in your being? You wish you could say yes, but I doubt it.

However, how deep does your relationship with God grow when life seems to get the best of you? Very deep! This is when you call out to Him and become desperate for His intervention. You go to Him on a daily basis and wait on Him. Without His intervention, you think you cannot go on.

Yes, you guessed it: no pain, no gain. Our relationship with the Lord grows deeper, stronger, and truer in times of distress. I believe that is why the Lord sometimes allows us to experience the bottom of the pit. In times of desperation, we turn to Him and we are changed. It is in those times that we learn how much God really loves us. We learn to depend on Him and trust Him.

How we respond in times of distress and desperation determines our destiny. This is what the book is all about. No matter what you are experiencing, God wants to make you whole again. You will read testimonies in the beginning to encourage you. What God does for one person, He will do for all. This I know because God does not favor one person over another.

After being encouraged, your journey from ashes to beauty begins. I encourage you to take time to really think about what you are reading. Take time to be honest with God, your situation, and ultimately yourself. Allow His Word to transform your heart, mind, and life. Your destiny awaits you. Let's begin.

SECTION ONE

ACTS 10:34, "AND PETER OPENED HIS MOUTH AND SAID: MOST CERTAINLY AND THOROUGHLY I NOW PERCEIVE AND UNDERSTAND THAT GOD SHOWS NO PARTIALITY AND IS NO RESPECTOR OF PERSONS."

~ Chapter 1 ~
My Story: Broken by a Past
The Beginning of a Ministry

I grew up in a household with a father, mother, and two sisters. Being the baby in the family, I was spoiled. I can say that now, but back then I would have argued to my grave that I was not treated differently. My father was a truck driver and I really only saw him Thursday through Sunday. I loved my father. I loved working outside with him in the garden and doing chores with him. I know that he loved me, but he was not very affectionate.

My mother was a very loving person. She was overly eager to please others, so I got my way most of the time. My sisters were wonderful. I got along great with both of them; when one would be mad at me, the other one would stick up for me. It was such a plan!

My paternal grandmother strongly encouraged our family to go to church, so we all went to church every week. She loved the Lord. If I did not go to church on Sunday, I had to call Grandma and tell her why. So, trust me, I went to church!

We lived in a small rural town and everyone knew each other. I loved school, running, and acting like I was a real estate agent (that was my mother's profession). When something began to happen to me, I began to change.

I was sexually abused. It happened four or five times and then stopped. I questioned who I was and was there something wrong with me? In order to deal with it, I acted like nothing ever happened and went on with my life. This was easier than trying to figure out why it happened.

The feelings of guilt and shame did not come right away, but slowly developed. What would happen if others found out? This was when I discovered I could wear a mask and no one would find out. If I acted

perfectly and was great at sports and received great grades, no one would ever question if something bad had happened to me.

It was only a couple of years after that when my parents began to argue and fight. It was horrible. The tension in our home could have been cut with a knife. I remember secretly praying at night that my parents would get a divorce because hearing them fight was difficult for me. To my surprise, my parents did separate and then ultimately divorced.

After my parents' divorce, my mom and I moved away to a large city. My oldest sister was already out of the house, and my middle sister lived with my dad. Our family was no longer a cohesive unit. I lost the support of my sisters. All my family stayed in the small town except my mother and me. I did not realize the impact a divorce had until I was living it. However, learning to wear the mask earlier in life helped because I loved school and sports and was also voted best girl athlete in eighth grade. The mask covered the pain again. Or did it?

It got to the point I could no longer hide the pain, and I became a very angry teenager. I turned to dating and drinking alcohol at a very early age. I can remember being a freshman in high school and getting intoxicated on a few occasions. Instead of telling someone how bad I was hurting, I held it in and began a descent into painful decisions.

I was angry at myself for getting into situations that turned from bad to worse. Anger seemed to beget more anger. I found myself never getting relief from the anger, and depression began to set in. At the time, I did not share with anyone what was going on. I would even go to youth night at a friend's church, but no one seemed to tell that I was hurting. I do not know if I was really good at hiding it, or if no one wanted to go there.

I began to drink on most weekends when alcohol was available. I can remember drinking to decrease the anger, depression, loneliness, and feelings of fear. I would be home late at night by myself and I would be terrified. In bed with my Bible, I would cry myself to sleep at night. The feelings were overpowering.

My mom and I would rarely speak. It amounted to my telling her how much I hated her and it always ended up with her crying. I was

very good at hiding the way I felt. Or was I? No one seemed to see my pain and I was able to continue to wear a mask.

In high school, I was an overachiever, getting good grades and being on the dance line. I wanted everyone to notice me and sought their approval. Everyone seemed to love me and I was always the life of the party. I figured if I was picture-perfect on the outside then no one could see the pain on the inside.

No one knew what was going on in my heart, mind, and feelings. However, I was able to move on with my life because I began to turn back to God. I obtained my master's degree in social work, had a successful career counseling people, and had good relationships with all of my family members. From the outside, I looked like I had it all and was passionate about helping people.

However, every time I would counsel someone regarding sexual abuse issues, I would come home and find myself being angry. I began to allow God to go to that dark place in my life. I was able to forgive the people who had hurt me and allow healing in those areas, but only to a certain extent.

I learned it was easier to forgive others than it was to relinquish myself from the decisions I had made when I was in such pain. I remained angry at myself for putting myself into situations that caused more harm. Guilt and shame were the issues that held me in bondage.

I "should have" known better than to put myself in certain situations. I "should have" known better than to drink alcohol to cover the pain. I "should have" known all these things because, after all, I grew up loving the Lord. Do you get the picture? I had forgiven the people who had actually hurt me, but I could not extend the same forgiveness and grace to myself. It always seems hardest to forgive oneself.

I began to cry out to God to help me. I wanted to like all of myself. I wanted to know the blood of Jesus could wipe away my past. For eight months, I cried out to God by praying, reading my Bible, and going to church. I knew I was saved and going to heaven, and I would share the love of Christ with others, but I could not let go of my past.

Until, one day, it happened. I was fall cleaning (like spring cleaning, only in the fall) and was listening to the Christian radio station. All of a sudden, I heard the words, "Your sins are as far as the east is from the

west." A dam burst open and the grace of God flowed to me in such an overwhelming sense that I fell to my knees and wept.

It had broken! I now knew the grace that covered the dark place in my life that once held me in bondage. At first, I could not stop weeping. After a while, my weeping turned into shouting for joy. I am so glad I was alone because if someone would have seen me, they would have thought I'd lost my mind. I began praising God. I was FREE! I began dancing around my living room and felt like I had lost a hundred pounds.

When I began to realize what the freedom really meant, I sat down and started to pray. This was my prayer: "Lord, I know there are hurting people out there who are just like me, people who need to know Your forgiveness and saving grace. Lord, send me people who are hurting and I will tell everyone who will listen about You."

God began to change how I saw everything. Even the beauty of the flowers began to change. How I thought about God and Who He was changed. I no longer wanted to drink any alcohol. I remember telling my husband, "God is up to something. He is changing how I see everything."

In the fall of 2003, the Lord called me to begin Living in the Light Ministries. I then had an encounter with God that forever changed my life. His Spirit overwhelmed me and I felt this awesome power in my stomach. I could not eat, sleep, or quit feeling His powerful presence.

So, out of my past brokenness came my ministry, Living in the Light Ministries. I have been able to minister to many people and have witnessed many people accept the Lord, be delivered from guilt and shame, and become healed of emotional wounds. I have learned that what was my trial has become my testimony. What I thought was a mess turned into a ministry. Who would have thought that the girl who was hurting so much could bring a gospel of peace to a hurting world? The anger, pain, guilt, shame, and fear that held me for so long were now replaced with love, light, and life. The party girl had now become the ordained minister.

This is the Lord and Him alone. Nothing and no one else could have brought about complete deliverance. I tried to use alcohol, men, success, and things to take away the guilt and shame. But they could not. However, suddenly, an encounter with God changed my whole

life. I was free. Free at last! It took eight months, but it was well worth the determination not to quit.

I encourage you to keep pressing into God until you receive your deliverance. Your experience may be different. You may have been physically abused by your husband or raped by a boyfriend; however, the result can be the same: deliverance from guilt, shame, pain, anger, depression, loneliness, fear, or any other emotion you are experiencing. God is an awesome God! Just give Him the opportunity to set you free. Know that His desire is for you to live a life of freedom.

Be like David and myself by following Psalm 138:3: "In the day when I called, You answered me; and You strengthened me with strength (might and inflexibility to temptation) in my inner self." Cry out to God right now. He hears you. And He wants to respond!

~ Chapter 2 ~
Nancy's Story: Broken by Divorce

My life story begins in a small Midwestern town in the 1960s. I was a teenager in a typical family with loving parents and grandparents. I was the first-born and surely Daddy's sweet little girl with blue eyes and curly blond hair.

My mother and I were attending the local Assembly of God Church. We had heard that someone was coming to hold a revival at our church; he was well known as a powerful preacher and great musician. I loved music and was excited about this opportunity. His name was Jimmy Swaggart, and he came and drew hundreds of people to our church.

That night I made a commitment to serve Jesus. This experience changed my life. I tried to take all things to God. God says that He loves us and will take care of us. I felt happy and content with my life. You need to know this because as I later ran away from the Lord, I knew that He still chased after me. I believe that God always calls our name to return to relationship with Him.

Going to high school and making new friends was fun for me. But what was God's plan for my life? I wanted to become a teacher. I had applied for a state teacher's scholarship and God opened that door for me.

Living at home during my college years, I worked at a drugstore for extra money. My father and I would have late-night talks about solving life's problems after I would come home from my part-time job. He was a news reporter and I respected him greatly.

I had only dated some but, turning twenty-one years old, I decided I wanted to see what many other people were like. I started to

be too busy to attend church or read my Bible. I was constantly looking for someone special.

I met a man a few years older than me and he began to shower me with gifts and much attention. I fell madly in love and we were married the following year. We both graduated college and found good jobs. He became a CPA and I was hired as a first-grade teacher. Dreams and hopes of a great future were there, but we left God out of our lives.

My husband was very demanding and ready to start a family. Being immature, I felt trapped and that I had missed out on something. I was just beginning my teaching career and loved that. So after only three years, we separated and I filed for divorce. Being single seemed fun for a short while, but then shame, fear, depression, and anger became the norm. These emotional reactions made my life difficult.

Growing up in the church, I knew this was wrong. Divorce should not have been an option. I was so angry that God had let me make this big mistake. I was not able to acknowledge my own role in the failed relationship.

This was the beginning of the path filled with many poor choices. The only thing that I knew for sure was that God had led me to become a teacher. I cared deeply about my students and worked diligently to educate them, even while my personal life was a disaster.

Being close to thirty years old, I felt I needed a man to be happy. I met a kind and gentle man who fell in love with me. Everyone liked him and we became good friends and married. Money was not a problem in this marriage. We bought a nice home and a new MGB sports car. Our lives were very busy but not fulfilled. We purchased a boat and a summer home at Lake of the Ozarks in Missouri.

After a few years we separated and he waited patiently while I decided what I wanted to do with my life. I felt that he deserved a wife who loved and respected him. I was not able to do this. How could I have done this for him? I felt isolated and ashamed because I had married just to avoid being alone. Finally, I chose to file for a divorce. Yet divorce was one of those disastrous failures that happened to others, not to me. Until it did—twice! Being divorced violated a lifetime struggle to live up to God's standards. *What now?* I asked myself. I had

no answers. I was going through many relationships, trying to mask the loneliness with activities to keep busy.

One day at work I ran into a former classmate. She asked the question, "Where are you going to church?" "Nowhere," I said. She stated that she was very surprised at that. I was so ashamed because I grew up knowing how important church was. I kept beating myself up and repeating in my head, *I should have known better.* We continued talking and she invited me to come and sing in the choir at her church.

My thought was that this might be a good activity to occupy some time in my life. God was so good to send this lady to encourage me to take a path back to Him. So I went to choir practice and all these people were kind and loving. They truly loved the Lord, and reminded me of what I was really missing in my life—a daily relationship with Jesus. I sang in the choir for a few months before surrendering my will to His.

One Sunday morning, I ran down to the altar for healing from the pain of my past. I cried out to God and He did not reject me, even though He knew every part of my life. He showed mercy and compassion to me. I felt His loving forgiveness. He filled my emptiness with His presence. He forgave all of my failures. I felt clean from His holiness. When God wraps His arms around us, we come to a place of forgiveness that is filled with peace and rest.

He began to change my heart and transform my life. For the next six years, I began to develop a deep relationship with the Lord. I was content being single and put all my hopes and dreams in His hands. I knew that I could trust Him to meet all my needs. When I did this, He opened the storehouse of blessings in my life. I vowed to continue to pursue God with passion all the days of my life.

One year later, my father became very ill and was in a coma for thirty days. The doctors gave up on him but my mother and I did not. We felt that the Lord would not let him die without another chance to accept Him. We were there at the hospital praying daily and on the thirty-first evening, he woke up. The doctors were amazed that there was no brain damage at all.

Later that week he came home and began to read his Bible. My father asked Jesus into his heart, and he lived for God for two years before his death. Remember that God's timing is perfect. Keep believ-

ing in the power of prayer. In the years that followed, other family members have also come to know and serve the Lord. Praise God!

This just strengthened my belief that our lives are ordered by the Lord in a beautiful way for His glory. If you will only entrust Him with your life, He will order your steps. If you try to regulate your own life, it will only be amiss and a failure. Only God can successfully guide you.

Where you are in life is no surprise to God. The Lord knew that I would love to be married but was afraid to trust my feelings. So God sent a man who loved the Lord and wanted to be my partner in life. He made me feel special plus he appreciated what I brought to his life.

Our love grew and we were married. We put God as our source of life. God began to bless us all along the way as we served Him. Twenty-five years together and we are still deeply in love. My husband has placed me in the forefront of his heart and I respect him for the many good qualities that he has shown to me and others over the years. Helping at the local church has also been a joy for both of us.

Through the years, God helped us with many trials with family members, such as long-term illness, death, feuds, and a few divorces. When we were in our deepest grief and felt farthest from God, this is when He was really the closest. That is when we were most open to His restoring power.

The Lord was preparing me for the next phase of my life. Both of us being retired gave my husband and me time to relax and travel. We were living on a small lake and telling others about God's goodness to us. We enjoyed the security of the family of Christ and the close friendships that had developed at our church.

I was asked to teach a divorce care support class at church. My first response was, "No, thank you." I did not want to remember all the pain of my past mistakes. But I said that I would pray about it. Well, God reminded me that I was now full of His joy and that He would help me teach the class.

I learned that those who have been wounded most deeply can be blessed with the gift of helping others to heal. God is full of mercy for all of us. I began to have a dedication to help others start over and have a new beginning in their life. I felt that the Lord had chosen me to teach the divorce care class and I submitted my way to Him. I knew

that I could encourage others. I needed to tell people that Jesus would never leave them nor forsake them even while they were going through the difficult time of divorce.

The first class began with people whose dreams had been shattered and their lives filled with confusion. I told them that God's love can heal all of their wounds and bruises. My heart was broken for their souls.

As the weeks passed, I saw many people healed by emotional and spiritual stabilization. The Lord helped me talk about my mistakes in detail, without pain, to help others. As I sat before the Lord, each person's face came to mind and I felt the need to pray for that person. The Lord even woke me up in the middle of the night to give me an idea or remembrance to tell the class. God had a plan and destiny for each one of them and these people needed to be reminded of that.

After twelve weeks of class, many people began to trust that God was in control of their life. They felt precious to the Lord and remembered that God could give them peace and joy.

I have taught the class for three years, which has allowed many men and women to cope with separation or divorce. Most have grown closer to God, and many became optimistic that they would be able to have an amazing life in Christ. They began to find their fulfillment in Him alone.

I wrote my life story hoping that whoever reads my words will discover what really matters in life. Having a relationship with Jesus Christ is what you need. You can only have a peaceful life as a result of God-centered living. Only then will there be divine intervention in your life. The Holy Spirit can then work freely in you. I want to go through the rest of my life giving praise and honor to God. May this be your desire also.

~ Chapter 3 ~
Ken's Story: Broken by Cancer

Life was good. My wife and I were both working and enjoying all that life had to offer. We were living what some have called "the good life." We had what we wanted, when we wanted it. If there was something we needed, we bought it. If there was a place we wanted to travel, we traveled there.

We had wonderful children and grand children that we loved to spend time with. I had turned sixty and was feeling great. I even patted myself on the back for not being sick a day in my life.

I believed in God and Jesus, but was not really a believer. I knew there was a God and that Jesus had come to save me from my sins. That was about the depth of my relationship with God. I guess you could say there really was no relationship. Part of the reason for this is I had seen people who said they were Christians, but did not act like it. I judged God on how other's acted. This kept me from having a further relationship with God.

After Christmas in 2006, I became sick. I had gone to the doctors and was first told I had the flu. With further doctor's appointments, I was told I had the crud. However, I could not get rid of whatever was ailing me.

My family demanded me to see another doctor, so I made an appointment with a doctor at St. Louis University Hospital. The doctor examined me, took several vials of blood and told me to return April 23 for the results.

My wife, daughter, and son-in-law accompanied me on return to the hospital for the test results. My wife mentioned maybe we should go to the chapel which urged my son-in-law to ask if I had ever received Christ in my heart. I agreed to go to the chapel. My son-in-law led my

wife and me in accepting Christ in our hearts by saying the salvation prayer. I really accepted Christ in my heart and knew I was saved.

As soon as the doctor came in the office he asked if I had heard of leukemia. He told me I was dying from it and needed to be admitted to the hospital immediately. How quickly in one moment my life changed drastically. The carefree lifestyle and come easy attitude were gone. It is amazing how one day I felt so good and within a few months was told I had stage four cancer and only three to six months to live.

That night, April 23, the pastor from the church my son attended came to visit and pray with me. I could not believe he would drive all that way. I will never forget that night. Since I did not know how to pray, the pastor told me to just talk with God like I was talking on the phone with a friend. That night was the beginning of wonderful phone conversations with God. I learned how to pray and talk with God.

The most amazing thing happened. Even though I was given one of the worst diagnosis' possible, I knew somehow that God was going to heal me of the cancer. The next morning I already had an appointment at one of the top cancer center's in the United States. God was already working on my healing.

I was discharged on Wednesday April 24 and went to church that night. I went up to the altar for prayer and the pastor and other people surrounded me and prayed that God would heal me. Peace came that I would survive this cancer scare.

Treatment began quickly and I could sense that God was going to take care of me. My fears decreased and I placed my life completely in His hands. I prayed for my wife and family for strength and encouragement because my faith had increased and I wanted them to have the faith that I did.

I asked the doctor treating me if she believed in miracles. I told her, "I don't know if you do or not, but with God and your help, I am going to lick this." She said she would do her part, and my faith believed God would do His.

After the first and second cycles of treatment, the cancer took a major decrease and then stayed even. I knew that God was healing me. I was excited and began to tell everyone at treatment about God and how Jesus died for them. My faith was soaring and I felt good.

In August of the same year, just four months later, it went from good to horrible. I contracted a blood bacteria infection and had to cease treatment. I was in the hospital for ten days and actually almost died.

When I was released, the doctor stated further treatment had to be cancelled and there was nothing more she could do for me. I remember feeling fear rise in me. I could see the devastation on my wife's face and it caused stress in our marriage.

I want to comment on the fear that rose within me. I learned the devil is a liar. He would put thoughts in my head like, *you aren't going to survive this, God is not going to heal you,* and *what are you going to do now?* I knew if I allowed these thoughts to continue I would be done fighting.

I like to say that Satan is a mouse. If he can get his head in, then he is going to come in and mess your mind up. To keep him out of my mind, I read my Bible everyday, had others pray for me, prayed myself, attended church as often I as could, and participated in a life group at church.

When I returned home, I was so weak. I had to use a walker to move around. I quickly learned that I could not feel sorry for myself. I could not think about giving up. This was a perfect time for me to allow the cancer to take over and quit fighting. However, I knew that was not an option for me.

If you find yourself in this position right now, do not give up! One thing I learned about myself was I thought I had reached the worst part when given the cancer diagnosis, however it got worse. I knew I had to tighten my belt, so to speak, and fight harder. I was determined!

The doctor scheduled another CT scan to follow up on the progression of the cancer. There was a Jamaican worker that held my hand and stated he was going to pray over the CT scan and bless the results. I was amazed at his statement and my faith increased.

Three weeks later I returned for my follow up appointment with the doctor and all the fluid was gone and fifty percent of lymph nodes that were positive for cancer were either cancer free or greatly decreased. Once again, God was healing me. I knew nothing is impossible for God, no matter what the doctor said. I want to encourage you right now if you are going through this. It would be great if doctor's at

religious hospitals allowed room for miracles, but if your doctor does not, do not let that discourage you. I believe more people would survive cancer if they just believed in God as their healer and did not rely solely on their doctor's opinion. Miracles do happen and yours may be next.

The cancer has come and gone multiple times. I am not sure why God allows this to happen, but I just think to myself *maybe this is God's way for me to talk with more people about Him.* So when I go for treatment, I take scripture cards and coins with me. I tell other people receiving treatment Who God is and how He loves them. I also share how Jesus died for their sins. I ask to pray with them and am pleased when people say yes.

Knowing I am like everyone else, when the cancer returns, fear is the first emotion I experience. Remember how I said if you can keep the devil out of your head you can overcome anything? This is one of my main focuses. Every time the cancer returns, I have to quickly get my mind on God.

I can remember one day I went up to the altar for prayer after the cancer had returned. I had my eyes closed and I felt someone grab me around the waist and I felt them pick me up. I felt a sensation go through my body and I knew that God was healing me.

After prayer, I asked a friend who I knew prayed for me, "Who picked me up?" He replied, "No one." I shared with my friend what I experienced and I knew that God had once again touched my body. I went back to the doctor and the cancer had decreased and almost gone away.

There is one thing I know, God is faithful! Every time I have needed a healing, it happened. Every time I call out to God, He hears me. Every time fear comes to my mind, His peace eases it.

These last five years have been difficult on my wife and marriage. When the cancer returns, fear also rises up in her mind. We pray together and realize we both have to quickly get refocused on God. I have learned that she needs to go to work and spend time by herself to work through her own thoughts and a good support group of Christian friends to pray with her and for her.

I continue to read my Bible, pray, go up to the altar at prayer time if needed, and participate in my small group. I have friends who I know are praying for me and a loving family and wife that are always there for me. Currently, the cancer returned and was five centimeters by seven centimeters, but within just a week, it decreased seventy-five percent again.

There is not enough room to write all the thoughts and fears that have occurred because of the cancer. However, there is one thing I know, God is my healer. I had to do my part of not giving up and leaning completely on Him and He continues to do His part of taking care of me. There have also been people who have helped me throughout this time.

If my testimony can help one person find God, then every thing I have gone through is worth it. If you are reading this and you have been diagnosed with cancer, be encouraged. I know how you feel. I know the days that I was exhausted and felt sorry for myself and wanted to give up. But you can't! You have to continue to fight and be determined that nothing is impossible with God.

My determination has caused me to say "I will see my youngest grand daughter graduate from high school" and she is only in grade school right now. I know that some day I will die, but not because of cancer. I made my mind up that the devil was not going to control my thoughts. I would rather be gone and have treasures in heaven then be on earth with the devil.

~ Chapter 4 ~
Kraig's Story: Broken by Life Changes

I had been married for around eight years and loved my wife. We would do a lot of fun activities and most of the time it included hanging out with friends. We had built our second home and life was going well.

We had changed churches due to my wife having an experience with God that changed her life. I handled the change, but began to have issues with how my wife was changing.

My wife quit going out dancing and drinking. I was not upset about her stopping drinking because it had caused a few problems in our marriage. However, when she no longer wanted to go out dancing, that was difficult for me. I enjoyed dancing, and it was one of the ways I exercised. I began to feel betrayed, lost, and unconnected to my wife.

"What is going on?" was one of my main questions. I began to feel sorry for myself and became angry at my wife. She was no longer the woman I married. I could not get beyond how having an experience with God could change a person so much. She was changing and I had no say anymore.

I want to say that not every change was bad. She became more loving, considerate, and kind. She would often think of me before herself. I liked this change, but was so overwhelmed by the other changes that anger toward her was the norm.

In addition to the changes above, she quit her private counseling practice to go into full-time ministry. What? I could not believe it. We did not even discuss this as a couple. She had made the decision based on the leading of the Lord without taking into consideration how I felt about it. I was angry, confused, and felt helpless so I began to push her away.

I wish that was all that had occurred, but it got worse. To add to the changes, she stated she felt led by the Lord to travel to Winston-Salem, North Carolina, to hold healing and miracle services. I really wanted to support her, so I traveled with her to host a luncheon with some of the pastors in that area. This pushed me over the edge emotionally.

I was angry at her changing. I was jealous of the relationship between her and God and felt like God was "her new man." I was scared because I was not sure what was going to happen to our relationship. I was confused at why God would lead her to do these things if I was not in agreement. I began not sleeping well, which led me to become anxious.

After the luncheon in Winston-Salem, I could not let anything go anymore. I would lash out at her with unkind words and was just becoming more upset. My nice life that I thought would last was now at a crossroads. I knew something needed to change or this marriage was going to be over.

A friend came over one day and we went fishing. It was a good time and I enjoyed focusing on something else. It was windy that day, so windy that I ran out of battery and we had to oar back. I had gone up to the house before my friend did because he was putting up his fishing gear in his car and I wondered if he had tied the boat up.

That night, I woke up in the middle of the night and was struggling emotionally. I was feeling very sorry for myself and hit rock bottom. It was four-fifteen in the morning and a thought came to my mind: *Is the boat tied up?* I went downstairs to look outside and the boat was not there. I became concerned because the fishing poles, battery, trolling motor, oars, and life jackets were still on board.

I looked over the lake and did not see the boat. I went outside with a flashlight and looked in the cove on the east side of our home. I figured this was where the boat had gone since that is usually the way the water moves. However, the boat was not there.

I then figured it was at the other end of the lake. I figured everything was stolen out of it so I went inside. I was now really feeling sorry for myself. My next thought was, *What am I going to do?*

Since I was feeling worried about the boat and a loss of what to do with my wife, I began talking to the Lord. I needed help and I needed it now! I got down on my knees and started praying. Once I stopped praying, I looked out over the lake again. There was a full moon, so the lake was very visible.

I could see the lake from the moonlight and between the shadows from the trees. I thought I saw a boat close to the other side, across the lake near the bank. The water was still and the wind was calm.

I went outside to get a better look. The boat began to move toward me. It got close enough to me and I could see that it was mine. How was this boat moving toward me without wind? How did it get to that side of the lake? Questions were coming to my mind.

However, so was a sense of peace. The boat was moving horizontally toward me and I could see that everything was still in it. The motor, battery, poles, life jackets, and oars were all there. A miracle in itself.

The boat kept coming toward me as I was standing next to the dock. When the boat was about ten yards away, all of a sudden, it turned parallel with the dock. I was shocked. It had turned and was coming into the dock just the way that I usually steer it. I bent down, grabbed the rope, and tied the boat up. This whole experience occurred in a thirty-minute time span.

I felt relieved and I thanked the Lord. I knew it was God. There was no other way! Through this miracle, the Lord let me know that my wife was following His leading. I knew that what my wife was doing was supposed to be. It helped me realize that instead of fighting against the changes, I needed to support them.

This experience helped me see that there really is a God and that God can and does do miracles. I do not know why I was so surprised that God showed up for me that night, but I was. I now realize that an experience with God can change a life. As a matter of fact, it should change a life.

I wish I could say that this miracle kept me from ever doubting again, but it did not. My wife continued to step out in obedience with preaching and praying for others. One day she came home after being part of a prayer room for healing and shared that she experienced a

person's arm growing during prayer. Once again, I doubted and told her so.

About three weeks before this, I had injured my toe while playing kick ball with family and friends and had been limping around all day. So when she shared her story, I said, "If God can do that then pray for my toe to be healed." She prayed for about fifteen seconds and then said, "Amen" and walked away. I said, "That's it?"

Later that evening, I was walking down the stairs and realized my toe did not hurt and had not been hurting. Once again, God showed up. This time, He healed me. I know this seems like such a small incident, but it taught me that God cares about every little detail of my life. God was speaking to me in ways that I understood Him. I now share with others my testimonies and tell them the importance of believing in Jesus and how He cares about everything going on in their lives.

I know that my wife is called to preach, write, and help others. I am thankful that God showed up and gave me peace. The situation could have resulted in a divorce had I not cried out to Him for help. I am thankful that I listened to Him through the boat miracle instead of trying to write it off as anything else.

I am thankful that God continues to show up every time I need Him. There have been other times that I have experienced anxiety that have been difficult but, through prayer, God helped me. He is the answer to every problem and the help to every situation.

I love to praise God and worship Him. I share with my family and friends what God means to me and has done for me. Even though some of them do not believe in Jesus, they believe in miracles being possible. This is at least a beginning to their relationship with Christ. I may not preach or write, but I do my part by telling others about Christ in my life.

If you are having a difficult time right now, stop and pray. God met me when I needed Him the most, so I know He will meet you. He will speak to you. The best part for me was God spoke to me in my language. He knew I would understand Him when He used the boat. What is your language? God will speak to you in a language you can understand. God does not speak the same way to everybody. How is

He speaking to you? Could it be through these words? Listen and hear what He is saying.

God has changed my life and He can and WILL change yours. Keep reading! I am proud to state that my wife is the author of this book. It is difficult at times stepping out in faith with her, but God leads and we follow.

~ Chapter 5 ~
My Testimony: Broken by Ministry

I had been preaching at churches and women's events, and had become ordained. I was in full-time ministry and kept stepping out as the Lord would lead me. I had seen the Lord perform marvelous and miraculous things. People were being healed of back problems, cancer, and other ailments. People were being delivered of guilt and shame for past failures, depression, anxiety, and addictions. People were being encouraged and uplifted, and words of wisdom and prophesy would flow. I knew I was in the center of God's Will for my life.

I knew the Lord was leading me to a three-day prayer and fast. During this time, I felt the Lord leading me to plant a church. I prayed about it, and the Lord had confirmed it. I talked it over with my husband and we agreed I would take the next step. I went to church-planting boot camp for a week.

This was the most difficult task God had led me to do, and He has led me to do some pretty difficult tasks. I began to build the budget. God showed up in a tremendous way and we met our budget quickly. I was off to the city to proclaim the good news of Jesus Christ. I was terrified, excited, and burdened all at once. I was more curious, though, about how God was going to make it all happen.

It began on such a difficult note. I went to a zoning meeting to try to get zoning changed on a specific building and was persecuted by about ten residents of the city. Wow! This really threw me back. However, I had complete peace during this meeting. I wanted to run and hide, yet God gave me every word to speak. I realized this was going to be a battle but I rented another little office and away we went.

In the very first Bible study, a woman rededicated her life to the Lord and was filled with the Holy Spirit. During my time in the

city, there were more than eight people saved, two filled with the Holy Spirit, and three people healed of physical ailments. However, the church plant was an emotional rollercoaster. I prayed and fasted so often and waited for God to move. After all, God had called me to plant this church; He would establish it! I gave my all for the church but, unfortunately, it never got off the ground and we had to close the office.

I felt like I did in 1993 when my mother and I lost everything in the flood. I remember taking a boat to my home and only seeing one inch of the roof. At that time, knowing I had lost everything was so overwhelming. Do you know the feeling of working so hard for something, putting your whole life into a situation then losing it all? That was how I felt in 1993 and it was how I felt about the church plant.

I had prayed, fasted, talked with people, invested financially, and staked my reputation on the church plant. Just to have it all come tumbling down was more than difficult to say the least. Losing all my hopes and dreams for ministry was devastating. The hopes and dreams were what motivated my life. What was going to happen now? Could I ever recover, was my question?

Since I felt like I had lost everything in a career or ministry perspective, this led to more problems and more questions. I began to have major problems spiritually. The question that kept going through my mind was, *Why would God ask me to do something He knew would fail?* I couldn't wrap my mind around God actually setting me up to fail. Have you ever had this thought? This was how I was feeling and couldn't help but begin questioning myself and if I really knew the direction of the Lord. I had prayed and fasted so often and poured my whole being into the church plant. I was really confused, somewhat angry, and began to doubt my ability to hear the Lord.

The Lord in all His grace led me to Matthew 23:37. This scripture talks about how Jesus lamented over Jerusalem and stated, "O Jerusalem, Jerusalem, murdering the prophets and stoning those who are sent to you! How often would I have gathered your children together as a mother fowl gathers her brood under her wings, and you refused!" I felt the Lord was revealing to me that His plan was for a church, but the people of that city had free will and that I had not failed. While the

scripture had brought some relief, I still struggled. I began to doubt my ability to recognize God's voice and leading.

Because of this came all the other issues about ministry like, "This is too hard"; "God, why didn't you leave me alone in my private counseling practice, where I was helping people?"; "I can't do this anymore!"; "I don't know if I want to do this anymore." I knew God was awesome, powerful, and almighty. Remember, I had seen the miraculous. God was on His throne! *But was He?* began to be my question. This had rattled my faith.

I asked, "God, why couldn't you make people respond?" "People have free will" came to my heart. Just like God would not make people in that city respond, God would not make me stay in ministry. I stepped away from my daily devotions, praying and fasting times, and my focus on ministry. I had to take a break!

Since the church office closed, I had to obtain other employment. Ministry that I loved so dear ceased, and I went back into the social work field full time. This placed the added stress on me of looking for a job, going on interviews, and trying to figure out what I was supposed to be doing—all the while questioning myself and feeling like a failure.

Prior to the church plant closing, my husband and I had begun building a new home. This proved to be much more difficult than we imagined. My husband, who does home improvement projects as a business, had already built two other homes for us. This was the third and last home we were going to build. What started off as exciting turned into a living nightmare.

My husband, who is usually very laidback, became overly stressed. Now, it was not my husband's desire for me to be stressed also; however, when you love someone, no matter how hard you try, you suffer with them. I will never forget the morning that it had gone from bad to worse for my husband. You would think being a counselor I could have helped him. But I could not. I felt very helpless which made me feel, in addition to the church closing, that my whole world was crumbling and I was not sure about anything anymore. Have you ever felt helpless?

A spirit of fear was attempting to come over me. Thoughts kept coming to my mind: *What if I cannot help him? What if everything falls apart?* I will never forget the first night this happened.

All night long, I went back from the bathroom being sick to lying in bed with my whole body shaking. I was able to contact three women of God over the phone and email while this was happening. They all prayed for me and peace flooded my body and mind. However, after about ten minutes of peace, the fear and shaking would hit and I would cry out to God again and once again peace flooded my mind and body. This happened all night. I never did fall asleep. I literally felt like I was losing my mind!

I was spiritually drained, emotionally drained, physically drained, and I had hit bottom. With the church closing and my husband becoming too stressed, I could not handle anything else. I was just trying to survive each day. Thoughts of ministry were the furthest from my mind. I was just trying to get up in the morning, go to my new job, and pray for my husband.

Things began to look up for my husband when he went on an extended vacation in Florida to my mother's home. He just needed to get away from the stress of the new house. I was relieved that he was feeling better. However, this placed me into another quandary. I was now responsible for working a new job, building a home, and selling our other home, all the while dealing with the spiritual dilemma.

I was in survival mode and spiritually, emotionally, and mentally numb. The spirit of fear attempted on two other occasions to take over, but by the grace of God, His peace won the victory. I began to go back to the basics of life.

I began to know God on another level that I had never known. There was brokenness in me that was deeper than anything I had ever experienced. I was so raw in every area of my life. I was so overwhelmed by the tasks in front of me that I literally quoted the Word of God all day long. Even though I had issues with God about ministry, I knew He was my strength and saving grace! I knew without Him, I would have never made it through those four months.

With everything my husband and I went through, it made our marriage stronger and there is rawness to our marriage now that had never been there before. We both know that God was our deliverer, healer, and sustainer for those months.

As I mentioned in the introduction, with pain comes growth. I am sharing this testimony to tell you that this book has come from those four months of desperation. Have I figured everything out ministry-wise? No. Do I understand why God sent me to that city? Not really. Do I trust that God will always be there for me? ABSOLUTELY!

Even in my darkest hours, God never left me. I can remember singing praise and worship songs every day. Those songs got me through those difficult days when all I wanted to do was cry, hide, or run away. His Word literally became my food for the day.

Since that time, during my quiet times with God, I have asked Him the "why" questions: Why did I have to close the church plant and leave full-time ministry? Why did my husband have to become stressed? Why was He allowing bad things to happen? Here is what the Lord spoke to my spirit: "I never left your side throughout the whole time." I began to realize that everything I had gone through has brought me to a point of writing these words on this page.

God did not make bad things happen to me, but He allowed those things to happen to me. Just like you. God did not cause your husband to hit you or your parents to harm you. But out of the bad can come good. What the enemy meant for harm, God will turn into good for those who love Him (Romans 8:28).

The Bible says we go through things so we can comfort others who are going through difficult times. II Corinthians 1:3-4 states, "… and the God [Who is the Source] of every comfort (consolation and encouragement), 4 Who comforts (consoles and encourages) us in every trouble (calamity and affliction), so that we may also be able to comfort (console and encourage) those who are in any kind of trouble or distress, with the comfort (consolation and encouragement) with which we ourselves are comforted (consoled and encouraged) by God."

If I went through everything and can now share so you can gain the victory then it was all worth it. If you move from brokenness to beauty then God's Will is accomplished. The Bible says that we are to lay down our life for others, this is what my calling and ministry is all about: getting beyond myself, my suffering, my questions and "whys" to preach a message of healing, deliverance, and hope.

I continue to preach, but with more of a rawness and a passion. God continues to heal people physically and emotionally, and minister to those who are hurting. I continue to see miracles, signs, and wonders. However, when I see someone who is broken, I ask God for a specific scripture or word for that person. Something they can hold on to during the midnight hour when everything seems at its worst.

The Lord spoke Isaiah 61:1 to me in 2003, when He called me into ministry. One part of that scripture is, "To heal the broken hearted." I believe that is part of what I am called to do. And that is what I believe this book will do: heal the broken hearted.

I want to share a scripture that helped me. I lived on Psalm 91 for four months. I had read it before over and over, but now I trust it and live it out! As we begin to move forward in this book, nothing would be more appropriate than to recite Psalm 91:

1 He Who dwells in the secret place of the Most High shall remain stable and fixed under the shadow of the Almighty [Whose power no foe can withstand]. 2 I will say of the Lord, He is my Refuge and my Fortress, my God; on Him I lean and rely, and in Him I [confidently] trust! 3 For [then] He will deliver you from the snare of the fowler and from the deadly pestilence. 4 [Then] He will cover you with His pinions, and under His wings shall you trust and find refuge; His truth and His faithfulness are a shield and a buckler. 5 You shall not be afraid of the terror by night, nor of the arrow (the evil plots and slanders of the wicked) that flies by day, 6 Nor of the pestilence that stalks in darkness, nor of destruction and sudden death that surprise and lay waste at noonday. 7 A thousand may fall at your side, and ten thousand at your right hand, but it shall not come near you. 8 Only a spectator you shall be [yourself inaccessible in the secret place of the Most High] as you witness the reward of the wicked. 9 Because you have made the Lord your refuge, and the Most High your dwelling place, 10 There shall no

evil befall you, nor any plague or calamity come near your tent. 11 For He will give His angels [especial] charge over you to accompany and defend and preserve you in all your ways [of obedience and service]. 12 They shall bear you up on their hands, lest you dash your foot against a stone. 13 You shall tread upon the lion and adder; the young lion and the serpent shall you trample underfoot. 14 Because he has set his love upon Me, therefore will I deliver him; I will set him on high, because he knows and understands My name [has a personal knowledge of My mercy, love, and kindness—trusts and relies on Me, knowing I will never forsake him, no, never]. 15 He shall call upon Me, and I will answer him; I will be with him in trouble, I will deliver him and honor him. 16 With long life will I satisfy him and show him My salvation.

SECTION TWO

ZECHARIAH 4:6, "...NOT BY MIGHT, NOR BY POWER, BUT BY MY SPIRIT [OF WHOM THE OIL IS A SYMBOL], SAYS THE LORD OF HOSTS."

~ Chapter 6 ~
A Place Called Broken

There is a place where each person finds him or herself in their life at least one time. This place is called broken. This place is one of great pain, sorrow, and life-changing circumstances. Being broken does not happen often in our lives, but when it does, we are never the same. If you have been there, you know exactly what I am referring to. If you are there now, you are probably in tears as you read this.

Being broken is different for each person. No one is broken the same way or over the same exact things. You may be wondering why one circumstance broke you when another did not. You may be thinking, *How did I get this low or how did I let it take me this far or how did I get into this situation?* Rest assured, you are not going crazy. There is a reason some circumstances break you and others do not.

How does being broken feel? I do not think everyone experiences it the same; however, there are common emotions. These emotions are anger, betrayal, desperation, guilt, shame, apathy, wanting to give up on life, exhaustion, sadness, fear, confusion, sickness, depression, anxiety, and the list goes on and on. There are some days you know how you feel and other days you are not sure what you feel. Some days are filled with intense emotions and other days you walk around in a daze and feeling numb. There are swings in emotions from moment to moment and then there may be weeks of complete depression. The main point is that everyone does not respond the same emotionally and emotions will be different based on the progress and depth of your brokenness.

Now that the emotions have been identified, why does it happen? Many people have stated that God will break us. I do not think God breaks us. I believe God allows circumstances to happen. A lot of times it is because of the free will of other people. God will not control people and make them do what He wants them to do. Sometimes we are broken by our own behaviors. Another circumstance, such as an

illness, occurs because sin has entered the world. However, one thing I do know is that God never gives us more than we can handle!

As a therapist and with my own experience, I have identified three areas that need to be met in order for a person to be broken. This is the reason some circumstances break a person while others do not. This is also the reason some people can handle a similar situation and yet other people cannot seem to get beyond it.

ABILITY TO FUNCTION

The first area is the ability to function. The circumstances have to impact a person's ability to function normally. What do I mean by this? This could mean having to take medication to go to sleep or an increase in anxiety, where the blood pressure increases. It could impact the ability or desire to participate in activities, social gatherings, or hobbies. The impact does not have to be great. A small change is all that is needed.

Here are some more examples to help explain and clarify what I mean about the ability to function being impacted: when work becomes so stressful you feel like coming home and having a drink every night; when you cease hanging out with family because your husband becomes verbally abusive when you do; when your spouse no longer wants to be home because of the fighting; when you cannot sleep at night because your mind keeps playing the situation over and over.

We have all had circumstances in our life when we exhibited similar behaviors. But they did not necessarily lead to brokenness. We experienced these behaviors for a couple of days, weeks, or maybe even a month, but eventually we moved beyond them. However, if these behaviors continue over the long term, there is an increased risk of being broken when the next situation arises.

STATE OF DISARRAY

Secondly, the circumstances have to cause a person to be in a state of disarray. This means a state of confusion or disorganization. In order for circumstances to cause brokenness, a person must be unable to make sense of the situation. Confusion as to why, how, and what happened must be present.

If a person can make sense of the circumstances, it is easier to process what is going on and move beyond it. However, if a person struggles with understanding the circumstance then it is more difficult and sometimes impossible to wrap their mind around it. When this occurs, a person will begin to obsess over the situation in order to try to explain it or figure it out.

For example, when a spouse has an affair or abruptly leaves the marriage, this is very confusing. Even if the other spouse had no idea there was a problem, that person will try to figure out, *Why did I not know it, how did it happen, and what part did I play?*

Another example of confusing circumstances is a medical illness or sudden death. Why did God allow it to happen? This causes great pain and places people in a state of disarray.

An example that I hear often is, "Why did I not pay attention to the red flags that my boyfriend was abusive and controlling?" This leads a lot of women, and sometimes men, to blame themselves for abusive relationships.

There are many more circumstances that I could mention, but in order to save paper, I will move on. Just understand that when a person begins to become confused and move into a state of disarray, that person could be headed to brokenness.

SUBDUED AND HUMBLED

Lastly, the person has to be totally subdued and humbled by the circumstance. The person has been forcefully quieted by the situation. This means the individual cannot fix the situation right away or at all. There has to be a loss of control of the situation and admittance to that loss.

In other words, the wife cannot make the husband come home. The doctor cannot make the cancer go away and you have tried everything you can. Your friend has betrayed you and never wants to talk to you again. You cannot leave your marriage because if you do, you fear your spouse will find you and kill you. Your boss has fired you and you have been walked to your car by security. Your child dies in a car accident. The situation seems hopeless.

The important part of this is there has to be admittance or feeling on the person's part that they are helpless. There is nothing you can do about the situation. You cannot make the situation go away or change. And if you can impact the situation in any way, you cannot make it better right away. The person has to realize what is going on.

Have you ever been around someone who refuses to believe reality? The person who refuses to believe their spouse is having an affair. The person who is trying everything they can to change someone else. The person who refuses to believe a loved one has died. The person who refuses to listen to the doctor so they do not follow up with any treatment. These people are not usually in a state of disarray; however, they will have to face the situation eventually.

These are the three areas that need to be met in order for a situation to cause brokenness. I want to put it all together now with my trial to help you understand what it looks like.

First, when everything began to happen with the church plant closing, I pulled away from my daily devotions, prayer, and fasting times. Secondly, I was in a state of disarray over the church plant closing. I was very confused and did not understand why it failed or what I did wrong. However, I trusted that God had a plan. So I did not stay in a state of confusion very long. I was humbled and knew I could not change the situation, but I trusted God. Therefore, the church plant closing did not cause me to become broken even though I felt like a failure.

However, when my husband began to become stressed, I was already halfway to brokenness. So when I could not change the situation regarding him, I became broken. When I knew I was helpless over my husband, that was the last straw, so to speak. Yes, I trusted God, but the situation was more than I could handle in addition to the church closing and my having to begin full-time secular employment again.

Does this help you understand what you are going through? Does this help you see how one situation may not cause you to be broken but, added with another, it breaks you? Or how one situation alone has caused you to become broken? Does it help you see why one person can become broken over the same situation and another person not?

I want to become very practical at this point. You have been given information about what leads to brokenness and how a person arrives there. However, this does not help the brokenness decrease or go away. Understanding is only part of the healing.

Here is a list of suggestions if you are currently broken. This list will help you begin to deal with what is happening right now. This list is not exhaustive, and is meant to help you from a counseling perspective.

1) Spend twenty minutes a day by yourself praying, meditating on God's Word, just being still, or going to church.

2) Ask others to pray for you and with you. At this point, you may not know how or what to pray. It is always encouraging to know that others are praying for you and that you are not alone.

3) Only tell a few close friends or people you can trust. Do not share your situation with too many people. This will help decrease gossip, confusion between different people giving you their opinions and advice, and having to retell the story, which can intensify or prolong the pain.

4) Go easy on yourself. Be nice to yourself. The enemy wants you to self-destruct. Realize that you may not be able to do everything you need or want to do. Do not add commitments to your schedule that are in addition to other activities you already have planned.

5) Only focus on important things at this time. Do not get caught up in the little things of life at this point. No one cares if you wore that same outfit to church two weeks ago. Pay your bills, go to work, and take care of the children. These are the important things.

6) Make sure you are getting enough sleep. Try to go to bed at the same time every night. Get into a routine of washing your face, brushing your teeth, changing into your pajamas, and having some quiet time. Getting enough rest will help with your ability to function and think.

7) Eat healthy meals. Make sure you are eating well and getting nutrition. This means if you are unable to eat because your stomach is upset, drink Ensure or something similar to

make sure you are getting nutrients your body needs. Lack of nutrition can cause headaches, which in turn makes you feel worse.

8) **Exercise if you are able.** This does not mean you have to exercise for at least one hour a day, but for any amount of time. Take a walk, go for a bike ride, go for a run, play volleyball, or lift weights. The important point is to burn off excess energy and to help clear your mind.

9) **Do one activity a week that you really enjoy.** This could be taking a drive to your favorite park, going to a movie, taking a bubble bath, or eating at your favorite restaurant. This will help you keep a sense of balance and joy.

Before I end this chapter, there is one more area that needs to be addressed. When a person is broken, they will make a choice. This is a major decision that will impact the length of time one is broken. Have you noticed how some people are broken for shorter periods of time than others? Sometimes it is because the situation begins to improve; however, most often, it is because of a choice that the person has made.

What am I referring to? I am referring to the choice to run to God or away from Him. I shared in my personal testimony that when the church plant closed, I ceased my prayer and fasting times and my daily devotion. This was an initial reaction to run from God.

However, when my husband started to become stressed, I immediately ran to God. I knew that He was the only answer to the situation. My choice to run to God was the best one I could have ever made. Did it make the situation go away? No. Did it make the pain stop? No. Did it deliver my husband? Not right away.

So why did I say that running to God was the best choice? Because in the middle of pain, sorrow, and confusion; peace, trust, and love shone through. God was with me. I was never alone. If you are feeling alone right now, run to God. Give Him your anger, hurt, confusion, and pain. His shoulders are big enough. He will meet you right where you are.

When King Jehoshaphat saw that a multitude of people were coming against him, he could have run into hiding. He could have come up with a battle plan all on his own. But how did he respond? II Chronicles

20:3 states, "Then Jehoshaphat feared, and set himself [determinedly, as his vital need] to seek the Lord; he proclaimed a fast in all Judah."

King Jehoshaphat ran to the Lord. He instructed all the people to fast and pray with him to the Lord. What was the response of the Lord? II Chronicles 20:14-15, 17 states, "Then the Spirit of the Lord came upon Jahaziel son of Zechariah...15...The Lord says this to you: Be not afraid or dismayed at this great multitude; for the battle is not yours, but God's. 17 You shall not need to fight in this battle; take your positions, stand still, and see the deliverance of the Lord [Who is] with you, O Judah and Jerusalem. Fear not nor be dismayed. Tomorrow go out against them, for the Lord is with you."

The Lord responded by fighting the battle. What was the outcome? II Chronicles 20:29-30 states, "And the fear of God came upon all the kingdoms of those countries when they heard that the Lord had fought against the enemies of Israel. 30 So the realm of Jehoshaphat was quiet, for his God gave him rest round about." God took care of the battle and then gave King Jehoshaphat rest.

> God can do the same for you. Let God fight your battle and give you rest. I know what God did for King Jehoshaphat and for me. He can do it for you! God does not love me more than you. God does not like me more than you. He loves all of us and nothing can ever separate us from that love (Romans 8:35-39). NOTHING!

So make the best choice you can and run to God. What are you waiting for? Put down the book and run to Him right now. Just say, "God, I need You! I cannot get through this without You. Help me right now. Forgive me for running away." When you do, I know God will be right there with you.

I addressed the choice of running to God or away from Him. In II Chronicles 20:3, King Jehoshaphat called for a time of prayer and fasting when they had a battle ahead of them. I encourage you to make the decision to run to God. Be like King Jehoshaphat and run to God. Psalm 50:15 states, "And call on Me in the day of trouble; I will deliver you, and you shall honor and glorify Me."

~ Chapter 7 ~
Finding Peace with God

Now that you have run to God, what do you do next? Calling out to Him is a necessity, but what happens if you are angry at God? Have you ever been angry at God? Have you ever been offended by God? Have you ever asked the "why" questions? Have you ever said, "Why me? God, why didn't You stop this? Why haven't You healed me?"

This is why so many people come in for counseling. People become stuck asking the why questions. Being able to move beyond the why questions is imperative.

I would love to be able to share with you that I have never asked these questions. However, I have. I have asked them in different situations and been angry at God. I have to admit I have even been offended by God. I am glad I did not remain angry or stuck on these questions, but I think it is human nature to respond this way initially.

We are not perfect and do not need to try to hide our feelings. God has big shoulders and can handle us coming to Him with our hurt, anger, frustration, and confusion. Think about David before he became king. Read the Psalms that he wrote and you will quickly see that he ran to God with all of his feelings, good and bad. Keep in mind that David was the one who God said, "Was a man after His own heart" (Acts 13:22). If God approved of David sharing everything with Him then you can, too.

KNOW HIS LOVE

You are now at the point where you have run to, or you have been running to, God and crying out to Him. GREAT! Do not leave this spot. This is the time when you really need to know how much God loves you. When I was broken, I had a very difficult time realizing how much God loved me. I thought my circumstances revealed a different character of God. How could God say He loved me when I was hurting so bad?

The enemy is the father of all lies (John 8:44). The enemy, who is the devil, wants you to think that God has left you and question God's love for you. Have you asked yourself, *How could He really love me if He let this situation happen?* The enemy will allow you to think that God is good, but maybe not to you or not all the time. What thoughts has the enemy put in your head about God? What thoughts keep you from having peace with God?

If you noticed in the testimonies given, there were thoughts of *I should have known better.* Cognitive therapy focuses on what a person believes about themselves or the situation. This in turn determines what a person will think. When someone begins to think certain thoughts, then their emotions are triggered. When emotions are triggered, then perception of experiences will be based on their preconceived beliefs. It all begins with what you believe.

If you believe positive things about yourself, you will have more positive thoughts about who you are and what you are capable of doing. If you believe negative things about yourself, you will have negative thoughts about who you are and how you cannot do certain things.

In an effort to meet me right where I was, God led me to Romans 8. I have read this chapter many times and it always encouraged me. However, on that day, the words literally jumped off the page into my heart.

Romans 8:35-39 states, "Who shall ever separate us from Christ's love? Shall suffering *and* affliction *and* tribulation? Or calamity *and* distress? Or persecution or hunger or destitution or peril or sword? 36 Even as it is written, For Thy sake we are put to death all the day long; we are regarded *and* counted as sheep for the slaughter. 37 Yet amid all these things we are more than conquerors *and* gain a surpassing victory through Him Who loved us. 38 For I am persuaded beyond doubt (am sure) that neither death nor life, nor angels nor principalities, nor things impending *and* threatening nor things to come, nor powers, 39 Nor height nor depth, nor anything else in all creation will be able to separate us from the love of God which is in Christ Jesus our Lord."

These verses helped me to focus on how much God really does love me and increased my belief in His love. I had to be able to wrap my thinking around His love in order to find peace with Him. I HAD to know these verses in my heart. I knew them in my mind, but I had to know them in my heart. You do, too. You have to know how much God loves you.

Do you believe God loves you? We tend to view God's love for us how we were shown love by our earthly father. Did you receive love from your earthly father? If yes, then it makes it easier for you to accept and receive God's love. If you never received love from your earthly father, it is more difficult to receive and know God's love. Read every scripture you can about how much God loves you. This will help you begin to internalize His love. Here is a list of other scriptures on love: Ephesians 3:17-19, 5:2, Proverbs 8:17, Romans 5:5, and John 15:9, 16:27.

I John 4:7-8 states, "Beloved, let us love another, for love is (springs) from God; and he who loves [his fellowman] is begotten (born) of God and is coming [progressively] to know and understand God [to perceive and recognize and get a better and clearer knowledge of Him]. 8 He who does not love has not become acquainted with God [does not and never did know Him], for God is love."

BE MINDFUL OF HIM

The next part of finding peace with God is to be mindful of Him. When you are broken, you are so wrapped up in what is happening to you that you do not pay attention to what happens around you or for you. This can be difficult when your mind is overwhelmed.

In order to be mindful of God, you have to be still. When you are broken, there is so much turmoil all around you. The turmoil may involve other people, your thoughts, your emotions, or your view of God. Your mind may not shut off. You may replay a situation or conversation over and over. The only way to become mindful is to shut off everything else but God.

Psalm 46:10 states, "Let be and be still, and know (recognize and understand) that I am God..." In order to shut your mind off to your brokenness, you have to be still. This may happen at bedtime or driving to work. I encourage you to be still as many times a day as is necessary

and available. The more times you can become still and know that He is God, the better.

How do you become still? Practice makes perfect. When first practicing to be still, you may want to have praise and worship music playing. This can help you become focused. You may want to have a devotion book to get you focused on a subject. You may want to read a Psalm to help you ponder the greatness of God. All of these activities will help you ease into being still.

Practice sitting in a comfortable chair, at a picnic table, or in a lawn chair and just be still. When your mind begins to fade to other thoughts, redirect them to how great God is. Keep focused on God. Spend five minutes at first and then as time progresses, remain still until you feel released to move on.

Being still can come in spurts. You may be able to sit for twenty minutes one day and on another day only two minutes. The important part is that you try. There will be times you feel led to sit still and other times you will sit still and sense nothing. Keep practicing and the ultimate goal is to be led by the Spirit.

This will be one of the times when peace flows like a river. I can remember driving to my new job and God's peace would flow over me. I would be still and know that He was with me. It was at these times that God would give me a scripture for the day to meditate on. Or God would give me a picture in my mind that He was holding my hand at that moment. Or He would lead me to do something that needed to be done. Or He would just strengthen me for the day. God knew what I needed, and when I was still and knew He was God, He would meet that need. Right there. Right then.

The other added benefit of being still was that I was able to recognize the areas that God was moving in. If I would not have been able to be still, I would have missed out on the blessings God was giving me. There were many blessings, but I had to take time to be still in order to recognize them as such.

When brokenness occurs, people tend to shut down to other people and anything else that does not pertain to their situation. They often miss out on how God is moving on their behalf because they

are so wrapped up in their pain that they cannot or choose not to see anything else.

I want to say to you right now: do not miss out on what God IS doing. God is working on your behalf, but you might miss the daily blessings if you are not still and know that He is God. In the stillness, you are able to see with eyes of hope and not eyes of pain.

Hebrews 13:5,6 states, "Let your character or moral disposition be free from love of money [including greed, avarice, lust, and craving for earthly possessions] and be satisfied with your present [circumstances and with what you have]; for He [God] Himself has said, I will not in any way fail you nor give you up nor leave you without support. [I will] not, [I will] not, [I will] not in any degree leave you helpless nor forsake nor let [you] down (relax My hold on you)! [Assuredly not!] 6 So we take comfort and are encouraged and confidently and boldly say, The Lord is my Helper; I will not be seized with alarm [I will not fear or dread or be terrified]. What can man do to me?"

God says He will not fail you or leave you helpless. He wants to help you. This is a MUST for you to know. You have to be mindful that God is with you right where you are. God is with you while you cry yourself to sleep. He is with you as you drive to work. He is with you while you clean your home. He is with you while you take a walk. He is with you when someone else is threatening to harm you. It is very important that you are mindful that God is always with you.

When you are mindful that God is with you then you can say, "He is my helper; I will not be seized with alarm." You know you can make it through the day when you focus on His presence. When I was going through my brokenness, these words would roll off my tongue and strengthen me: "I don't live by what I feel but by your truth. You are holding on to me."

Knowing that I was in the palm of God's hand was very comforting. I knew He was with me. I want to encourage you to focus right

now on how God is with you. Put down the book and just focus on Him holding your hand. God will not let go of you; don't let go of Him!

Matthew 11:28-30 states, "Come to Me, all you who labor and are heavy-laden *and* overburdened, and I will cause you to rest. [I will ease and relieve and refresh your souls.] 29 Take My yoke upon you and learn of Me, for I am gentle (meek) and humble (lowly) in heart, and you will find rest (relief and ease and refreshment and recreation and blessed quiet) for your souls. 30 For My yoke is wholesome (useful, good-not harsh, hard, sharp, or pressing, but comfortable, gracious, and pleasant), and My burden is light *and* easy to be borne."

God says come to Him and He will give you rest. But you have to be mindful of God in order for Him to give you rest. You have to know that He will give you not just physical rest but emotional and mental rest. Sometimes when you are going through a time of brokenness, it is the mental and emotional symptoms that keep you up at night. Getting your mind to "shut off" can be difficult. Begin to praise God and focus on Him and you will be given rest. This may not come quickly but, with practice, it will come.

TRUST HIM

Another major aspect to finding peace with God is learning to trust Him. Jeremiah 29:11 states, "For I know the thoughts *and* plans that I have for you, says the Lord, thoughts *and* plans for welfare *and* peace and not for evil, to give you hope in your final outcome."

You have to trust that God knows what is happening and that He will turn it around. God knows when you hurt and He knows what is ahead of you. When you are going through something difficult, it is hard to think about what lies ahead. You are so wrapped up in the moment that you cannot see what God has down the road. This is the time you have to trust that God has a plan for your life.

It was hard for me to look ahead and trust that God really had plans for me. What could those plans be? How could what was happening to me be for my welfare and peace? All I saw was evil winning out. Once I moved beyond that, I could see how God was moving. He is moving me to write down these words for you.

Do I believe that God broke me? Absolutely not! But God allowed it to happen to get me to a place where I could minister to others who are broken. His plan all along was for me to minister to hurting people. There is now a depth to me that was not there before.

I know it is hard for you to see right now how you will ever make it through, but you will. You will be able to look back and see how you made it through the fire and are stronger for it. God has a plan to use you someday because of your brokenness. Trust that He has you and will not let you go. Trust that you will make it through what you are experiencing right now.

Psalm 126:1-3 tells us, "When the Lord brought back the captives [who returned] to Zion, we were like those who dream [it seemed so unreal]. 2 Then were our mouths filled with laughter, and our tongues with singing. Then they said among the nations, The Lord has done great things for them 3 The Lord has done great things for us! We are glad!" God delivered the Israelites and He can and will deliver you. As God moves, it may seem unreal at first, but like with the Israelites, laughter and singing will return. You can trust Him!

~ Chapter 8 ~
God Will Fight for You

Another important understanding is that the battle belongs to the Lord. You do not have to figure out how you are going to get through the situation or how other people are going to change. This is not the time to think you have to figure everything out. I know for me, I would spend hours thinking about what to do next or how to rectify the situation. However, I found myself being emotionally and mentally exhausted. I learned that God wanted to fight for me and I had to allow Him to. God wants to fight for you. He wants to take care of you. You have to allow Him to fight for you.

Acts 6:10 states, "But they were not able to resist the intelligence *and* the wisdom and [the inspiration of] the Spirit with which *and* by Whom he spoke." This is when Stephen began to share about Jesus to the Pharisees. The Pharisees became angry because they could not handle hearing the truth. When the Spirit is at work, nothing can stop Him.

When God is on your side, He will give you words to speak to people. God will give you favor with whom you need it. The Spirit will work on your behalf. Trust this!

I have written already about King Jehoshaphat and how he turned to God when surrounded in battle. It seemed there was no way out. II Chronicles 20:15, 17 states, "He said, Hearken, all Judah, you inhabitants of Jerusalem, and you King Jehoshaphat. The Lord says this to you: Be not afraid or dismayed at this great multitude; for the battle is not yours, but God's. 17 You shall not need to fight in this battle; take your positions, stand still, and see the deliverance of the Lord [Who is] with you, O Judah and Jerusalem. Fear not nor be dismayed. Tomorrow go out against them, for the Lord is with you."

God wanted to fight for His people in His way, on His terms. God wants to do the same for you. Allow Him to fight for you! I have already touched on this part, but you need to be still and allow God

to fight. If you are always trying to figure it out or change it then your situation will take longer to resolve. Many times people get in God's way of doing what needs to be done and this prolongs everything. Are you doing this? Are you in God's way?

So what happened to King Jehoshaphat? II Chronicles 20:18-29 tells the rest of the story. In order to save paper, I will summarize. After the Israelites received the Word of the Lord, they praised God. Before the army went out, they sang praises to the Lord. The Lord showed up and won the battle without their help and then all those in the land feared Him. Then they were given rest.

The lesson? When you allow God to fight the battle, He will! You just need to be still and hear what He has to say to you. Then praise Him until you see the breakthrough. Your situation will change, but only once you trust God to battle for you. If you try to fix the situation yourself, it will only make matters worse.

I have seen people take matters into their own hands because the pain is so overwhelming. Remember, I have been there so I know the pain of being broken. You may be able to lessen your pain temporarily, but in the long run you will end up worse off because God has a plan of deliverance.

Ephesians 6:11-13 states, "Put on God's whole armor [the armor of a heavy-armed soldier which God supplies], that you may be able successfully to stand up against [all] the strategies *and* the deceits of the devil. 12 For we are not wrestling with flesh and blood [contending only with physical opponents], but against the despotisms, against the powers, against [the master spirits who are] the world rulers of this present darkness, against the spirit forces of wickedness in the heavenly (supernatural) sphere. 13 Therefore put on God's complete armor, that you may be able to resist *and* stand your ground on the evil day [of danger], and, having done all [the crisis demands], to stand [firmly in your place]."

The battle is the Lord's. You need to put on the armor of God because people are not your problem. You may think it is your spouse,

child, or boss. In reality, it is evil that is in charge. Your spouse, child, or boss is allowing evil to work through them. It is not them personally that the battle is with. This is why it is so important to allow God to fight for you.

I know God was fighting for me when I was still and would see little things taking place. I refused to fight with my husband because I knew he was not the problem. I needed to allow God to fight the battle and I stayed on my knees in prayer. I also knew that the devil was fighting against me regarding the church plant. I could not become mad at the people in the city, but pray for them.

The enemy wants you to become mad at people. He wants you to blame people and hold resentment, bitterness, and anger so he can get a grip in your mind and heart. This is an attempt to ruin your life. However, when you recognize what is really happening, you can battle on your knees and allow God to handle the real battle.

When you recognize who the fight is really with, this will allow you to have peace with yourself and others. When you refuse to allow anger to continue then not only will you have peace with God but peace with other people.

Having peace with others at this point is very crucial. The last thing you need right now is to have arguments. You may find yourself being less tolerant of people, but remember they are not your problem. The thief comes in order to steal, kill, and destroy (John 10:10). Remember that the enemy wants to keep you in pain and destroy your life. Don't let him! Have peace with people!

The benefit of having peace with others is that you end up having peace with yourself. Have you ever left an argument with someone and become upset with yourself because you didn't hold your tongue? I know I have. Now is not the time to add issues and feel guilty. The more peace you have with others, the more peace it will bring you.

Finding peace with God really is the first step to healing. You cannot be healed without having peace with the Healer. If you have peace with Him then continue reading the book. If you still do not have peace with God, I encourage you to re-read the last two chapters. Pray and ask God to help you identify what is keeping you from having peace with Him. Are you still angry at Him or offended by Him? Allow the

Spirit to speak to your heart and mind, and direct you to the area that you need to address in order to move forward.

This is not to say you will never ask God questions, but hopefully you are at a place where you have been still and know that He is God. You know that He is your only answer and you are leaning, trusting, and relying on Him.

This does not mean that you will do everything right. You will still struggle with wanting to battle for yourself. You may struggle with anger, resentment, and bitterness. You will become exhausted and need to enter His rest again. Remember to go easy on yourself. You are NOT perfect. Do not expect yourself to act perfectly. You are still struggling and need guidance.

Peace flows like a river. Allow the peace of God to flow to you. Let go of your anger toward God and do not be offended. Know He loves you more than anything. Be mindful of every blessing, great and small. Be still and know He is God. Enter His rest. Trust Him. Allow Him to fight for you. Lastly, having peace with God brings peace with others and yourself.

Can you feel His presence? Christ is interceding for you right now at the throne of God. The first step to healing is to find peace with God. What is the next step? Keep reading.

~ Chapter 9 ~
Identifying with Christ

Hopefully, you are beginning to experience peace and rest. You may still not understand and questions may remain. You still search and have a difficult time with what is happening to you and are emotionally overwhelmed. Now is the time to begin to identify with Christ.

We have a God Who understands what we go through. If you take a look at the life of Christ, you will begin to understand that life was not easy for Him either. I think sometimes, as Christians, we think our life should be easier than the norm. This is because we trust God and know how powerful He is, yet for some reason, we still have problems. John 16:33 informs us we will have problems, but that Christ has overcome the world. When you identify with Christ, you can overcome anything.

THE LIFE OF CHRIST

Looking back at the life of Christ is the place to start. Philippians 2:6-8 states, "Who, although being essentially one with God *and* in the form of God [possessing the fullness of the attributes which make God God], did not think this equality with God was a thing to be eagerly grasped *or* retained, 7 But stripped Himself [of all privileges and rightful dignity], so as to assume the guise of a servant (slave), in that He became like men *and* was born a human being. 8 And after he had appeared in human form, He abased *and* humbled Himself [still further] and carried His obedience to the extreme of death, even the death of the cross!"

Jesus was in heaven in all His glory before He came to earth. He left the ease of heaven and gave up all privileges to come to earth. He could have stayed in heaven, where angels were singing His praises, but He chose to come to earth and save the lost. Jesus chose the hard road because of His love for you and me. I think it is very important to ponder this thought.

Before you can identify with Christ, you have to realize what He gave up for you. I truly believe it is easier to identify with some-one whom you know suffered for you than it is to just know ABOUT someone. You have to believe that Jesus came for you.

After Christ came, He grew physically, like you and I do. He had parents and siblings and probably had to do chores. We know that He was a carpenter, so He worked. He did not sit back and expect to be waited on.

The Bible does not tell us much about the childhood of Christ, but we begin to receive an account when he presents Himself to the Jordan River. Matthew 3:13-17 tells of the story of Jesus being baptized and how the Spirit of God descended upon Him and how a voice from heaven spoke and stated, in verse 17, "This is My Son, My Beloved, in Whom I delight!"

Can you imagine this scene? I would have loved to have been there! Here is the first experience with Jesus beginning His purpose—and what a beginning! Nothing like this had ever occurred before. God sure does know how to introduce His Son!

However, read the very next verse. Matthew 4:1 states, "Then Jesus was led (guided) by the [Holy] Spirit into the wilderness (desert) to be tempted (tested and tried) by the devil." Can you comprehend this? Jesus was just introduced in grand style and then was led to the wilderness to be tested and tried.

I find it interesting that God would allow this to happen. If Jesus was not beyond testing and trying, why do we expect anything less for ourselves? Let me answer that for you, because we are human and think from our own perspective. Before Jesus had a public ministry, He had to be tested and tried by the devil. If you are a Christian, you will be tested and tried. Do you notice it was not God Who tested and tried, but the devil? God just allowed it to happen. However, He overcame the devil.

Jesus went through so much in His life on earth. He was rejected, physically hurt, lonely, betrayed, had family issues, was called a liar, suf-fered emotionally, and his actions were defended by no one. He had to constantly explain Himself and people would not listen. His disciples would not even pray with Him, but would fall asleep because they were

more concerned about themselves than they were about Him (Matthew 26). People constantly wanted to trap Him or physically kill Him.

Do you feel any of these things right now? Have you been betrayed? Have you suffered emotionally? Are you lonely and hurt? Have you been hurt physically? Does your spouse not listen to you and would rather spend time at the bar or with another woman? Have you been rejected by someone that you love? Have your parents harmed you, when they were the ones who were supposed to protect you? Have the people you were called to minister to not responded to you? Has your life not turned out the way you thought it would?

Hebrews 4:15 states, "For we do not have a High Priest Who is unable to understand *and* sympathize *and* have a shared feeling with our weaknesses *and* infirmities *and* liability to the assaults of temptation, but One Who has been tempted in every respect as we are, yet without sinning." We have a God Who understands. You can identify with Christ. He has been through, in some way, shape, or form, what you are going through right now. You can identify with Him!

I love the next verse. Hebrews 4:16 states, "Let us then fearlessly *and* confidently *and* boldly draw near to the throne of grace (the throne of God's unmerited favor to us sinners), that we may receive mercy [for our failures] and find grace to help in good time for every need [appropriate help and well-timed help, coming just when we need it]."

When you identify with Christ, you can then boldly cry out to Him in prayer and ask for help. He knows what you think and feel. Go to Him and allow His grace to help you. You will find help in your time of need—not just any help, but appropriate and well-timed help. And the help will come just when you need it!

When I was physically sick from being upset, I can remember crying out to God. I asked Him to help me right then and there. Did Jesus ever experience that overwhelming feeling I felt? I can picture Jesus praying with sweat like drops of blood from His brow because of what He was about to endure. This brings about a sense of trust for me. If Christ experienced that, then I can identify more easily with Him.

⭐ God knows that you will have trials and tribulations and He knows how much you can handle.

> I Corinthians 10:13 states, "For no temptation (no trial regarded as enticing to sin), [no matter how it comes or where it leads] has overtaken you *and* laid hold on you that is not common to man [that is, no temptation or trial has come to you that is beyond human resistance and that is not adjusted and adapted and belonging to human experience, and such as man can bear]. But God is faithful [to His Word and to His compassionate nature], and He [can be trusted] not to let you be tempted *and* tried *and* assayed beyond your ability *and* strength of resistance *and* power to endure, but with the temptation He will [always] also provide the way out (the means of escape to a landing place), that you may be capable *and* strong *and* powerful to bear up under it patiently."

Many people focus just on this scripture that God does not give us more than we can handle. I really believe that God is good and is with us in our time of need. There are times we go through that we cannot get through on our own. But He always gives us the way out: Him. Calling out to Him is the way we endure.

However, I want to take it further. When we encounter times of brokenness, the devil comes in and puts thoughts and lies in our head in order to attempt to change what we believe. When the devil can change what we believe; then our thoughts, feelings, and actions will become more negative. We begin to think about doing things we would normally not do just to get by.

The second part of Hebrews 4:15 is that Jesus was without sin. I know you are hurting right now. This is not the time to be making bad decisions and allowing temptation to overcome you. I Corinthians 10:13 states that God provides a way out. He is the way out! You have to continue to hold on to Him.

Throughout all the pain, turmoil, and suffering, continue to make right choices. Ask yourself the question, "What would Jesus do?" This

is the time to overcome evil with good (Romans 12:21). Identifying with Christ also means identifying with His suffering from the perspective that He remained without sin.

I know I wanted to run away from God at times, more in the beginning with the church plant closing. I did cease some of my time with Him. I would still pray, but at the most crucial time I tended to pull away instead of draw closer. I am glad that changed.

However, I want to encourage you right now. If you have pulled away even slightly, ask God to forgive you and draw near to Him again. Keep drawing near! The world does not have your answers. The bottom of the bottle does not hold your peace. The arms of another person do not bring vindication. The smoke from the drug does not help you see clearer. Are you getting my point? The grass is not greener on the worldly side than it is on God's side. The worldly way may bring immediate relief but causes more trouble down the road.

YOU ARE A CHILD OF GOD

Another way to identify with Christ is to realize you are a child of God. John 1:12 states, "But to as many as did receive *and* welcome Him, He gave the authority (power, privilege, right) to become the children of God, that is, to those who believe in (adhere to, trust in, and rely on) His name." You are a child of God. Even if you have felt that you never belonged anywhere, you have been given power, privileges, and certain rights because you are a child of God.

Identifying with Christ bestows on you this power, privilege, and right. If you do not identify with Christ, you will never know the benefits. I am not trying to make light of the benefits of being a child of the King of Kings, but am emphasizing that you have to grasp on to faith and trust to receive these benefits.

When you grab hold of these benefits, you can hold your head higher in confidence and know that it is just a matter of time before your situation changes. I can remember driving to work and thinking, *God will eventually change things.* I would have peace because I knew that God was going to work it out for my benefit. However, I would never have known that without grasping in my mind that I was the daughter of the King.

Romans 8:15-18 states, "For [the Spirit which] you have now received [is] not a spirit of slavery to put you once more in bondage to fear, but you have received the Spirit of adoption [the Spirit producing sonship] in [the bliss of] which we cry, Abba (Father)! Father! 16 The Spirit Himself [thus] testifies together with our own spirit, [assuring us] that we are children of God. 17 And if we are [His] children, then we are [His] heirs also; heirs of God and fellow heirs with Christ [sharing His inheritance with Him]; only we must share His suffering if we are to share His glory. 18 [But what of that?] For I consider that the sufferings of this present time (this present life) are not worth being compared with the glory that is about to be revealed to us *and* in us *and* for us *and* conferred on us!"

Awesome! You are an heir to the throne! That means every need you have has already been filled. Your need of love: met. Your need for protection: met. Your need for a friend: met. Your need for stability: met. Your need for forgiveness: met. Your need for healing: met. God shall supply your every need (Phil 4:19). Any need you have the kingdom of heaven will meet for you!

Identify with Christ and even though your problems may not go away, you know you are taken care of. Stop and think about it. If you are a parent, don't you want to give your child the world? Don't you want to protect them, love them, and provide for them? God is your Father. He feels the same way. Hebrews 2:18 states, "For because He Himself [in His humanity] has suffered in being tempted (tested and tried), He is able [immediately] to run to the cry of (assist, relieve) those who are being tempted *and* tested *and* tried [and who therefore are being exposed to suffering]."

~ Chapter 10 ~
Christist Your Savior

Do you need to also identify with Christ from the perspective of His death on the cross covering your sins? Are you broken because of your own behaviors? Have you made poor decisions since being broken because the pain seemed too much to bear?

In John 8, we learn of the woman who was caught in adultery and the crowds wanted to stone her. The "important" people (scribes and Pharisees) brought this woman to Jesus and they wanted Him to give them the permission to stone her and were testing Jesus to see how He would respond. I love how Jesus responds; verse 7 states, "However, when they persisted with their question, He raised Himself up and said, Let him who is without sin among you be the first to throw a stone at her." Jesus could have said, "Well, you guys are right, go ahead." But instead, He responds with, "You are free to stone her if you have never sinned."

Do you understand what this scripture truly says? No one is perfect and we all fall short of the glory of God (Romans 3:23). There are people who try to make you feel guilty because of what you have done or said. But I want to assure you that they have also sinned. John 8:11 states, "...Jesus said, I do not condemn you either. Go on your way and from now on sin no more."

Jesus reveals His true character here. He knows you have not been perfect and have done things while you are hurting, but He says He does not condemn you for these things. That is why Romans 5:8 states, "But God shows *and* clearly proves His [own] love for us by the fact that while we were still sinners, Christ (the Messiah, the Anointed One) died for us."

 ## ACCEPTING FORGIVENESS

Even though you may have brought on the situation yourself, if you identify with Christ from this point forward, God can and will

bring restoration in your life. That does not mean everything will turn out the way you want, but it does mean that He is with you and will not leave you.

Luke 13:2, 3 states, "And He replied by saying to them, Do you think that these Galileans were greater sinners than all the other Galileans because they have suffered this way? 3 I tell you, No; but unless you repent (change your mind for the better and heartily amend your ways, with abhorrence of your past sins), you will all likewise perish *and* be lost eternally." Your sin is not "worse" than anyone else's.

God used a murderer, adulterer, tax collector, and prostitute. If God can forgive and use these people, God can forgive you. Do not let the enemy keep you from believing that what you did was unforgivable. First, call out to God and ask for His forgiveness.

The part that is most difficult is when others refuse to forgive. Even though God forgives and He is the most important person, others may continue to remind you of what you did. When this occurs, you cannot make the person forgive you. You need to apologize. Then if the person still refuses to forgive you, you need to tell them there is nothing else you can say except that you will not repeat the behavior. You need to follow through and not repeat the behavior. When this occurs, then forgiving becomes their issue, not yours. People sometimes take longer to forgive you, but at least know that the blood of Christ can and will cover your sins.

Psalm 103:9-12 states, "He will not always chide *or* be contending, neither will He keep His anger forever *or* hold a grudge. 10 He has not dealt with us after our sins nor rewarded us according to our iniquities. 11 For as the heavens are high above the earth, so great are His mercy *and* loving-kindness toward those who reverently *and* worshipfully fear Him. 12 As far as the east is from the west, so far has He removed our transgressions from us."

God will not and cannot hold your sins against you once you confess and ask for His forgiveness. God is not mad at you and will not give you what you deserve because He is a loving God. Your sins are as far as the east is to the west. There was a time in my life when I had to pray for eight months to realize this scripture. Pray today that you, too, can experience what this scripture speaks.

* when God forgives our sins, He also wants us to forgive ourselves!

How do you learn to accept God's forgiveness? First, pray and ask God to help you accept His awesome gift. Read every scripture on how much God loves you and how much you mean to Him. Make sure you cease the behavior you need forgiveness for. When you continue to repeat the behavior, it becomes more difficult to accept God's forgiveness. Realize you are not the only one who has ever done the behavior and God has been able to forgive others. When others do not want to forgive you, do not let their unforgiveness become your problem. Accept forgiveness from God and allow Him to work on the other person in your life.

I want to proclaim to you Acts 13:38, "So let it be clearly known *and* understood by you, brethren, that through this Man (Jesus) forgiveness *and* removal of sins is now proclaimed to you." Through belief and identification with Christ, your sins are now forgiven.

Romans 8:1 states, "Therefore, [there is] now no condemnation (no adjudging guilty of wrong) for those who are in Christ Jesus, *who live* [and] walk not after the dictates of the flesh, but after the dictates of the Spirit."

Since you are a child of God, you are no longer found guilty! You are acquitted of all crimes (sins) against you. You do not need to feel guilty or "beat yourself up" for behaviors that you have been forgiven for.

However, you can decrease the amount of times you need forgiveness by living and walking according to how God wants you to live, and not how your feelings want you to live. Once you realize your sinful behaviors, you have to change those behaviors. You have to stop doing things that bring you down and separate you from God. This is the area that some people get stuck in. I know. I have been there.

The devil puts thoughts in your head like, *You can't change, so just give up and give into it; You can never change; God has not rescued you yet, so you are justified in doing these behaviors; These things you do are not as bad as what other people do;* and, *You are hurting too bad to control your behaviors.* Have any of these lies come into your mind? Some of them pounded my thoughts until I spoke the Word of God against them.

Even though you are hurting right now, you do not want to compound your problems. Walk according to the Spirit. What does this

mean? Do what you know you need to do so you will not be in a cycle of guilt and shame. Do not allow your feelings to vote right now. Identify with Christ and the Spirit and you WILL feel better. Proverbs 10:25 tells us, "When the whirlwind passes, the wicked are no more, but the [uncompromisingly] righteous have an everlasting foundation."

DON'T LISTEN TO OPINIONS

Identifying with Christ also means *not* identifying with what others say. This is a time when many people may give you advice or may question how you are responding. People usually mean well, but sometimes they are mistaken. People have problems judging, especially other Christians.

Have you heard this, "What did you do wrong to bring on God's judgment?" "What did you do to make the person leave you?" I know when the church plant closed one of the things I was most afraid of was what other people were going to say to me. I had a dear friend who would walk around with me at my home church and protect me from people. I am so thankful for this. When people would question me, my friend would divert the question and swoop me away.

John 8:14,15 states, "Jesus answered, Even if I do testify on My own behalf, My testimony is true *and* reliable *and* valid, for I know where I came from and where I am going; but you do not know where I come from or where I am going. 15 You [set yourselves up to] judge according to the flesh (by what you see). [You condemn by external, human standards.] I do not [set Myself up to] judge *or* condemn *or* sentence anyone."

This scripture is right after Jesus stated He is the Light of the World and the Pharisees said His testimony was worthless because He could not testify on His own behalf. Part of identifying with Christ is realizing that not everyone is going to understand what is going on in your life. People did not understand Jesus, nor will everyone understand you. However, they will still try to tell you what they think is going on.

You will encounter people who mean well but have no clue. You will encounter people who think they know exactly what you need to do. You will encounter people who want to tell you what you have

done wrong. You need to not listen to them and continue to identify with Christ.

I love one part of the story about Jairus's daughter being sick and the servants told him to no longer bother Jesus because she had died. Mark 5:36 states, "*Overhearing* but ignoring what they said, Jesus said to the ruler of the synagogue, Do not be seized with alarm *and* struck with fear; only keep on believing." Jesus heard what the servants had told Jairus, but He ignored it.

That is my counsel to you. Ignore what people are saying and just believe that God has you in the palm of His hands. Identify with Christ as a son or daughter of the King! Remember when I encouraged you just to share with only a couple of people what is going on? This is the reason. You can listen to their counsel and advice. However, you always have to compare it to the Word of God. Make your decisions based on the Word and not only on what people say.

Now, I want to say something important here. You may be running around sinning and doing things that are just magnifying your problems. If you are, God will correct you. God may use a person to bring you correction.

II Samuel 12 tells the story of how David had sinned against God and Nathan was sent to reveal it to him. Verse 7 states, "Then Nathan said to David, You are the man!..." There are times when someone you love will bring a word of correction. I encourage you to hear that word and receive it. You are hurting right now and sometimes in denial of the part you played. Do not get offended, but compare it to the Word and see if there is some truth to it.

WORD OF GOD

This brings me to the last part of identifying with Christ. You need to identify with the Word of God. If the Word brings correction, receive it. If the Word brings encouragement, receive it. If the Word brings favor, receive it. If the Word brings healing, receive it. If the Word brings deliverance, receive it. If the Word brings rest, receive it.

John 1:1 states, "In the beginning [before all time] was the Word (Christ), and the Word was with God, and the Word was God Himself." John 1:14 states, "And the Word (Christ) became flesh (human, incarnate)

and tabernacled (fixed His tent of flesh, lived awhile) among us…" When you identify with the Word, you identify with Christ.

Allow His Word to get down inside of you, to the depths of your soul. Base your decisions on the Word of God. Compare everything at this time to the Word. How does it compare? If the advice or counsel you receive is held up by scripture, then go with the advice. If it goes against what the Word says, then let the advice go and keep searching the scriptures for your answers.

When you identify with Christ, you identify with the King of Kings and the Lord of Lords. You cannot go wrong if you stick with Him! However, this does not mean everything will change immediately.

Have you identified with Christ? Have you asked Him to come into your life as your Lord and Savior? If you have never asked Him to come into your life and you would like to right now, pray this prayer: "*Lord, I admit I am a sinner. I believe that Christ died on the cross for my sins. I confess that I need Him every day of my life. Please come into my life today and help me. Thank you, Lord. AMEN*"

~ Chapter 11 ~
Life in the Word

At this time, you are searching for any area that brings hope. Hope is what keeps your eyes fixed on Christ. Hope is what keeps you putting one foot in front of the other. Hope is what you long for. Hope can only come from God. Hope comes when you know God's Word and promises.

Once you know God's promises, then you have to think on them. I know many people who have said they pray and call out to God but do not read the Bible. I often wonder how their hope increases and how often God speaks to them if they do not pick up the Bible and read what God has to say. God can speak through other people, hence this book. However, I believe the main way God communicates with His people is His Word.

AUTHORITY OF GOD'S WORD

II Timothy 3:16 says, "Every Scripture is God-breathed (given by His inspiration) and profitable for instruction, for reproof *and* conviction of sin, for correction of error *and* discipline in obedience, [and] for training in righteousness (in holy living, in conformity to God's will in thought, purpose, and action)." This is the main reason that reading God's Word is a whole chapter in this book.

You can trust that every scripture comes straight from God. If you do not know the above scripture, you may question the truth of some scriptures. This can cause confusion or lack of trust. Not only that, but some scriptures you read will lead you, while others will teach you, and still others will correct you. If you do not know that every scripture is from God, you will pick and choose which scriptures you want to believe. This will not help you or heal you.

THE POWER OF GOD'S WORD

Hebrews 4:12 states, "For the Word that God speaks is alive and full of power [making it active, operative, energizing, and effective];

it is sharper than any two-edged sword, penetrating to the dividing line of the breath of life (soul) and [the immortal] spirit, and of joints and marrow [of the deepest parts of our nature], exposing *and* sifting *and* analyzing *and* judging the very thoughts and purposes of the heart."

God's word is ALIVE! Do you need new life right now? Do you need to be revived? Yes, you do. The way to obtain this is to be in the Word of God. The Word will penetrate your heart. Sometimes this can be very uplifting, while other times it will mean you need to change some things in your life. However, every word is powerful and even if it is difficult to read, it will ultimately bring new life. I realized, in my brokenness, that in order to move forward at times, the Lord would have to correct my thinking. Yes, it was uncomfortable at times but since the Word is alive, when I recognized it, new life would result.

Psalm 119:50 states, "This is my comfort *and* consolation in my affliction; that Your word has revived me *and* given me life." I know in my time of brokenness, I needed to be revived. What is the best way to get revived? Reading the Word of God. Do not neglect this area but make it a priority every day to read the Bible. You will begin to see a difference in how you think and feel about your situation.

Jeremiah 1:12 tells us, "Then said the Lord to me, You have seen well, for I am alert *and* active, watching over My word to perform it." Not only does the Word of God bring new life and help revive you, but God watches over it that it will occur. None of God's Word will ever fail or fall to the ground without accomplishing that which it is sent to accomplish (I Samuel 3:19). This is a scripture that I quoted frequently to myself. It helped fight negative thoughts about things never changing. I would say, "God's Word never fails and it will accomplish what it needs to." After speaking this, my thoughts would become positive again and peace would return.

INCREASING FAITH

Hebrews 11:6 explains, "But without faith it is impossible to please *and* be satisfactory to Him. For whoever would come near to God must [necessary] believe that God exists and that He is the rewarder of those who earnestly *and* diligently seek Him [out]." I wanted to share this scripture to emphasize that God rewards people who are

willing to seek Him. The best place to seek God is in His Word. You have to believe that you will find God when you turn to Him.

If you believe that you will find God, you are more likely to read the Bible. If you have had problems in the past and read your Bible, then you already know that reading the Bible brings renewed life. However, if you have not had this experience, be prepared for strength to begin to rise in you.

Hebrews 11:6 not only addressed that God rewards those who seek Him, but it takes faith to believe that God can and will meet you right where you are. You are probably thinking, *Kristi, my faith is not real strong right now.* Or, *I really need to increase my faith but how do I do that?* I am so glad you asked this question.

Romans 10:17 states, "So faith comes by hearing [what is told], and what is heard comes by the preaching [of the message that came from the lips] of Christ (the Messiah Himself)." "From the lips of Christ Himself" is very important. John 1:1 says, "The word (Christ) was with God." John 1:14 says, "The word came and lived among us." Clearly, John was stating that Christ is the Word made flesh. So if faith comes by hearing the Words of Christ, then faith comes by reading the Word.

Faith increases when you read the Word of God. I cannot give you my faith. You cannot live off the faith of your spouse, best friend, parent, or pastor. You need to obtain and grow your own faith. I would be in awe at people's faith in the Bible and I found myself reading the most difficult stories to compare my situation to theirs and say to myself that if God can intervene in their life, surely He can intervene in mine.

Romans 4:3 states that Abraham's faith was credited to his account as righteousness. Righteousness means in right standing with God. Because of Abraham's belief in the promise God gave him about having a son, God stated that Abraham was in a right relationship with Him.

Romans 4:19-21 states, "He did not weaken in faith when he considered the [utter] impotence of his own body, which was as good as dead because he was about a hundred years old, or [when he considered] the barrenness of Sarah's [deadened] womb. 20 No unbelief *or* distrust made him waver (doubtingly question) concerning the promise of God, but he grew strong *and* was empowered by faith as he gave

praise *and* glory to God. 21 Fully satisfied *and* assured that God was able *and* mighty to keep His word *and* to do what He had promised."

I am astonished at how Abraham did not look at his and Sarah's physical bodies. I have to admit I would have, after waiting the first couple of years. To make it even more amazing, the scripture talks about Abraham's potency, which was as good as dead, and Sarah's womb, which was deadened. Even though their bodies were both "dead" (in the physical realm) to bear children, Abraham still believed. God was setting the stage, and we need to realize that He can do anything!

Abraham looked to God and no disbelief or distrust made him waver. Nothing was going to change his faith. This made him grow stronger and empowered him. This is the reason I am encouraging you to read the Bible. There is life in the Word!

Do you feel dead right now? Do you feel your marriage is dead or your dreams are dead? Follow the example of Abraham and let your faith rise. Let faith arise in you right now! As you read this, life is growing in you and you are becoming stronger! I know because, in faith, I believe that God is giving me every word to type and that it is well timed. If God can deliver on His promise to Abraham in a body that was basically dead then God can deliver on His promises to you!

RENEW YOUR MIND

Romans 12:2 states, "Do not be conformed to this world (this age), [fashioned after and adapted to its external, superficial customs], but be transformed (changed) by the [entire] renewal of your mind [by its new ideals and its new attitude], so that you may prove [for yourselves] what is the good and acceptable and perfect will of God *even* the thing which is good and acceptable and perfect [in His sight for you]."

Reading the Word will not only bring life but will transform and renew your mind. Why is this important? When your mind is renewed, you will know for yourself what God's Will is for your life. It is at this level that you will begin to know what you are supposed to do or how to move forward. Again, God's Word will teach you and lead you.

When you do not read the Word of God daily, your thoughts will begin to go down the wrong path and the devil will begin to tell

you lies about you and your situation. As you already know, when one negative thought comes, it brings many other negative thoughts with it. Before long, you again begin to feel overwhelmed, stressed out, and depressed. One way I know how to renew the mind is to read the Word of God! The devil is a liar and God's Word is complete truth. Which will you choose?

Isaiah 62:6 states, "...you who [are His servants and by your prayers] put the Lord in remembrance [of His promises], keep not silence." It is fundamental to the Christian faith to keep remembering what God has already done, what God is doing, and what God will do. The only way to keep remembering is to read the Word of God.

It is also important to recognize that is says, "Keep not silence." What does this mean? It means you need to talk about the promises of God. You need to speak them in your mind, in your heart, over yourself, and over your situation. I will touch more on this topic in the next chapter.

John 14:26 states, "But the Comforter (Counselor, Helper, Intercessor, Advocate, Strengthener, Standby), the Holy Spirit, Whom the Father will send in My name [in My place, to represent Me and act on My behalf], He will teach you all things. And He will cause you to recall (will remind you of, bring to your remembrance) everything I have told you."

There are many excuses why people do not read their Bible. People will say, "I forget what I read by the time I put the Bible down." This could be a great excuse except for the fact that John 14:26 defies that thinking. Jesus is telling His disciples that the Holy Spirit would remind them of what He spoke concerning things that were going to happen.

I know I had to make it a point to read my Bible daily. Otherwise, I would be too tired, could not focus, or too negative to want to read. And every time I was finished, I would feel much better and have a better outlook than when I started.

When you read the Bible, you may not remember what you read one hour later. However, when you need that scripture, it will come back to your mind. I can remember a time when the Spirit led me to read a couple of verses one morning before I even got out of bed. I read the scriptures and thought, *Well, those are wonderful scriptures.* I have to admit I really did not need them in that moment, or so I thought.

Hours later while I was sitting in the dentist's chair, sheer terror struck me. I cannot tell you why because I had never experienced those feelings before. Can you see where I am going with this? Yes, you guessed it. The scriptures I had read that morning came rushing back into my mind and I began quoting them (of course in my own words because I had not memorized them word for word). Within a minute or two, I was calmed back down and had moved beyond those feelings.

What you read will come back to your mind when you need it most. However, if you do not read the Bible, your thoughts will be more negative and it will be more difficult to focus on positive things. Yes, hearing the pastor's sermon might help something come to your mind. However, with the intensity of what you are experiencing, it is not enough just to hear a sermon one or two times a week and think that is going to bring your faith to a level that will overcome your brokenness.

The best way to begin is to look at the concordance at the back of your Bible or obtain a regular Bible concordance. Look up scriptures of promises you really need right now. If you are struggling with love, read scriptures on love. If you are struggling with fear, look up scriptures on fear. If you are struggling with forgiveness, look up scriptures on forgiveness. If you are struggling with feeling alone, look up scriptures that say God will never leave you. This is the place to start.

I do not usually recommend just skipping around the Bible but, right now, you need to know God's promises to you. You can take time to go back and read a book of the Bible one at a time or begin an in-depth study of something later; right now, it is focus time.

Once you begin to find scriptures that speak life to you, write some of them down on cue cards and place them all around your home, car, and office. I love visiting my sister because she has cue cards all over her home: on the bathroom mirror, refrigerator, and nightstand. When I get ready in her bathroom, I read. When I am getting something to drink from her refrigerator, I read. You can also carry them in your purse or wallet. Put them on your computer screen at home and work. Wherever you can think, place them there. Nothing is off limits.

Here are some scriptures that I feel led to write. There are so many more that will bring you life, but I want to begin the process for you in an effort to encourage you to take your reading the Word of God to a new level.

—-Philippians 4:19, "And my God will liberally supply (fill to the full) your every need according to His riches in glory in Christ Jesus." God can and will meet your every need; just bring it to Him!

—-Isaiah 53:5, "But He was wounded for our transgressions, He was bruised for our guilt *and* iniquities; the chastisement [needful to obtain] peace *and* well-being for us was upon Him, and with the stripes [that wounded] Him we are healed *and* made whole." If you need forgiveness or healing, then accept the death of Christ for your physical and spiritual healing.

—-Romans 8:37, "Yet amid all these things we are more than conquerors *and* gain a surpassing victory through Him Who loved us." Paul was emphasizing that nothing can ever separate you from the love of God. No troubles or trials will ever make God stop loving you. This is why we are more than conquerors.

—-Psalm 34:4, 7, "I sought (inquired of) the Lord *and* required Him [of necessity and on the authority of His Word], and he heard me, and delivered me from all my fears. 7 The Angel of the Lord encamps around those who fear Him [who revere and worship Him with awe] and each of them He delivers." God can and wants to deliver you. He encamps around you right now. Can you sense His presence?

—-Proverbs 18:24, "The man of many friends [a friend of all the world] will prove himself a bad friend, but there is a friend who sticks closer than a brother." If you are feeling lonely right now, know that Jesus is the friend Who is always right there with you. The Spirit lives inside of you. You are never truly alone! *I get lonely, but never alone!*

—-Philippians 4:6, "Do not fret or have any anxiety about anything, but in every circumstance *and* in everything, by prayer and petition (definite requests), with thanksgiving, continue to make your wants known to God." Take everything to God in prayer. Thank Him for what He has already done and allow Him to carry your burdens.

—-II Timothy 1:7, "For God did not give us a spirit of timidity (of cowardice, of craven and cringing and fawning fear), but [He has given

us a spirit] of power and of love and of calm *and* well-balanced mind *and* discipline *and* self-control." God did not give you fear! The devil is making you afraid. The Lord has given you power. You can overcome your fears with love and wisdom.

—-James 1:5, "If any of you is deficient in wisdom, let him ask of the giving God [Who gives] to everyone liberally *and* ungrudgingly, without reproaching *or* faultfinding, and it will be given him." If you need wisdom, ask for it! Ask God to help you. God wants you to walk in wisdom. Just believe and receive.

—-John 14:27, "Peace I leave with you; My [own] peace I now give *and* bequeath to you. Not as the world gives do I give to you. Do not let your hearts be troubled, neither let them be afraid. [Stop allowing yourselves to be agitated and disturbed; and do not permit yourselves to be fearful and intimidated and cowardly and unsettled.]" Jesus told us that He has given us peace. You already have it. You need to walk in it. The peace in this world is only temporary and more likely damaging. But the peace that Jesus gives is complete! Go to Him. I love how the scripture states for you to stop allowing yourself to be agitated and disturbed. I know, for me, my thoughts would go negative and if I did not quickly change them, I would become very stressed. Does this happen to you? Stop allowing it! Change your thoughts!

—-Nahum 1:7, "The Lord is good, a Strength *and* Stronghold in the day of trouble; He knows (recognizes, has knowledge of, and understands) those who take refuge *and* trust in Him." God is so good. Take a look around and see His blessings. He is also your strength and stronghold because He knows you. God knows you because you run to Him! Therefore, He will be your strength.

—-Psalm 91:1-2, "He who dwells in the secret place of the Most High shall remain stable *and* fixed under the shadow of the Almighty [Whose power no foe can withstand]. 2 I will say of the Lord, He is my Refuge and my Fortress, my God; on Him I lean *and* rely, *and* in Him I [confidently] trust!" When you dwell in the secret place, that means reading His Word, praying, and daily knowing His presence; you will remain stable. When you do that, then you can say (because you really know) that God is your fortress.

-Proverbs 3:5, *only* "Lean on, trust in, *and* be confident in the Lord with all your heart *and* mind and do not rely on your own insight *or* understanding." This scripture is so important when you are feeling broken. Do not rely on your own understanding because you may never understand. You may never figure it out and this will only frustrate you. Trust that the Lord has you in the palm of His hand and know that it is okay if you do not understand. *In all your ways acknowledge Him & He will direct your paths.*

—John 3:30, "He must increase, but I must decrease. [He must grow more prominent; I must grow less so.]" This scripture is when John the Baptist realized he needed to begin to back away and allow the ministry of Christ to be at the forefront. This is how it needs to be in your life. How you feel and what you think need to become less, and knowing the Word of God and His presence need to increase. Living for His Will in your life and not your own will needs to increase.

—-Isaiah 49:15, "[And the Lord answered] Can a woman forget her nursing child, that she should not have compassion on the son of her womb? Yes, they may forget, yet I will not forget you." God has not forgotten you, nor will He ever. You may feel like that right now, but know you will NEVER leave God's mind.

—-Hebrews 13:5-6, "...for He [God] Himself has said, I will not in any way fail you *nor* give you up *nor* leave you without support. [I will] not, [I will] not, [I will] not in any degree leave you helpless *nor* forsake *nor* let [you] down (relax My hold on you)! [Assuredly not!] 6 So we take comfort *and* are encouraged *and* confidently *and* boldly say, The Lord is my Helper; I will not be seized with alarm [I will not fear or dread or be terrified]. What can man do to me?" God clearly states that He will never leave you. When you really begin to know this scripture, you can then say, "He is my helper." You do not have to be afraid of what others may try to do to you. God is your helper. If God is for you, who can be against you? (Romans 8:31)

—-Hebrews 13:8, "Jesus Christ (the Messiah) is [always] the same, yesterday, today, [yes] and forever (to the ages)." Our Lord never changes. All the scriptures above are just as powerful today as they were the day they were written. You can trust in the Lord to deliver you. Just as He delivered me, He will deliver you. His love for me is the same as it is for you. Nothing can separate either one of us from God's love. Take courage and strength from knowing that God NEVER changes.

I encourage you to write down some scriptures on note cards and carry them around with you. When you need them, pull them out and read them. This will help keep your thoughts focused positively. The Word of God brings life. It can change your whole way of thinking.

~ Chapter 12 ~
Forgiveness

I pray that you are beginning to sense that you CAN overcome whatever is ahead of you. Your strength may still be waning, but hope is a companion that you have for a better tomorrow. In order to move forward, you need to keep taking steps forward. Forgiving others is a necessary step to wholeness.

You may not think you need to forgive anyone, but keep reading. Ask God to show you if there is anyone you need to forgive. Be open. Be honest.

THE IMPORTANCE OF FORGIVENESS

Forgiveness has not only played a role in my personal life, but also when I had my own private counseling practice. I did a study and found that eighty percent of my clients needed counseling due to not forgiving themselves or someone else. Eight percent needed to forgive themselves, fifty-two percent needed to forgive someone else, and forty percent needed to forgive someone else along with themselves.[1] What can be deciphered from these statistics? The lack of forgiveness leads to bondage.

How does this bondage affect your life? It will impact your emotions, thoughts, behaviors, body, and spiritual walk. When you refuse to forgive, you impact every area of your life. You will have more negative thoughts, feel more negative emotions, act more negatively, possibly have medical problems such as headaches or stomach aches, and your relationship with God will be hindered. Forgiveness begins with a choice, the choice to forgive.

I realize that as you are reading this, you may not be ready to forgive. You may have an "I deserve to be angry" attitude. If you have been hurt on purpose, then those feelings are real and normal. If your husband hits you or you have been raped, then you are justified in feeling this way. I am not saying that those feelings are wrong or not normal. However, those feelings are not healthy to keep. There comes

a certain point that, in order to move forward, you are going to need to pray and ask God to help you WANT to forgive.

This chapter is not intended to minimize what you have experienced or to invalidate your pain. Your feelings of anger, fear, shame, or betrayal need to be addressed and processed. However, I have been where you are and it is important to not remain stagnant or you will become stuck. Chances are you are stuck right now and that is why you have picked up this book and began reading.

You see the word "forgiveness" and you are probably thinking, *You surely cannot ask me to forgive the person or people who wronged me?* Yes, I am asking you to go to the place of tremendous pain and give it to the Lord. Read the whole chapter before you become mad, put the book down, and profess to never read it again. Let the whole truth of this chapter speak to you.

There are many scriptures on forgiveness. I believe it is because we find it so difficult to forgive. I believe the difficulty stems from our carnal, or human, nature. We want the person or people that hurt us to have to pay, or at least admit their wrongdoing and apologize.

Do you agree that all have sinned and fallen short of the glory of God? (Romans 3:23) Do you agree that you have not been perfect? Okay. Well at least we are in agreement thus far. No one is perfect and we all make mistakes. If we are honest, we know we have even intentionally said things or done things to make someone mad. Yes, I am even telling on myself. I have said things I knew I should not have just to push my husband's buttons.

Now that you realize you are not perfect, realize that sin is sin. One sin is not worse than another sin. Lying is a sin, just as gossip is a sin. Stealing is a sin, just as hating someone is a sin. Adultery is a sin, just as unforgiveness is a sin. You get my point!

I realize forgiveness is a process and can only be done with the help of God. What does forgiveness mean? Forgiveness means: 1) to let go of the pain and hurt that resulted from the situation, and 2) to also let go of wanting to punish the person or people who hurt you. So many people have professed forgiveness because they have moved beyond their pain, only to realize they still want to punish the person.

Have you seen families on television programs say they have forgiven their daughter's killer and even request that the murderer only receive a life sentence instead of death? We watch the program thinking, *I don't know if I could ever do that.* This is true forgiveness.

In Matthew 6, Jesus was teaching the disciples how to pray. This scripture teaches us, straight from Jesus, what to pray. Verse 12 states, "And forgive us our debts, as we also have forgiven (left, remitted, and let go of the debts, and have given up resentment against) our debtors." Jesus teaches the disciples to pray for the ability to help them forgive but connects it to our own forgiveness.

Why is it so important to forgive? Continuing after the Lord's Prayer, Matthew 6:14-15 states, "For if you forgive people their trespasses [their reckless and willful sins, leaving them, letting them go, and giving up resentment], your heavenly Father will also forgive you. 15 But if you do not forgive others their trespasses [their reckless and willful sins, leaving them, letting them go, and giving up resentment], neither will your Father forgive you your trespasses."

The bottom line? If you do not forgive the person or people who have hurt you, then God cannot forgive you. When you do not forgive, you have a broken relationship with God. Your prayers are not heard. Your peace is gone. This is the reason some people begin to look for peace in the world. Drinking alcohol may increase. Gambling may begin. Drug use may occur.

If you are doing any of these things, please realize that you are going in the wrong direction. You will not find true peace apart from God. The only peace that satisfies is God's peace.

If you refuse to forgive, your relationship with God is broken. Repent right now and ask God to help you. This is the first step to forgiveness. Just ask God to help you have the desire to WANT to forgive. Trust me; God will definitely answer that prayer!

It is easier to forgive someone if you know they made a mistake and did not intentionally mean to hurt you. However, you are called to forgive someone even if they were reckless and willful. Remember that sin is sin. If you are not at a place to forgive yet, begin to pray about it.

You may be thinking, *But how many times do I have to forgive this person? They have hurt me over and over.* Matthew 18:21-22 states, "Then

Peter came up to Him and said, Lord, how many times may my brother sin against me and I forgive him *and* let it go? [As many as] up to seven times? 22 Jesus answered him, I tell you, not up to seven times, but seventy times seven!"

Jesus knew this question would come up in our own minds. *How many times do I have to forgive my spouse, parent, child, or boss?* As many times as it takes! What we need to realize is that WE will need forgiveness more times than it will require us to forgive one person in our life. We sin on a daily basis and need forgiveness daily. Remember, all sin separates us from God.

It is important for each of us to forgive so our heavenly Father can forgive us. But I believe God also wants us to forgive because of other reasons—one being so the devil cannot obtain a foothold in our life. Remember, if you do not forgive someone else, then God cannot forgive you. This automatically opens a door for the devil to enter.

Ephesians 4:26-27 warns, "When angry, do not sin; do not ever let your wrath (your exasperation, your fury or indignation) last until the sun goes down. 27 Leave no [such] room *or* foothold for the devil [give no opportunity to him]." When you remain angry and do not forgive, you allow the devil to potentially control your life. What does this look like? Becoming cynical, judgmental, critical, and short-tempered are ways the foothold can manifest. Life is difficult enough without opening a door to allow the devil into your life. When this occurs, God cannot remove the devil until you repent.

You might be broken right now because you have refused to forgive and time has passed and your anger has grown stronger and stronger. Your marriage may have fallen apart partly because you would not forgive your spouse for something he or she did years ago.

Hebrews 12:14-15 states, "Strive to live in peace with everybody and pursue that consecration *and* holiness without which no one will [ever] see the Lord. 15 Exercise foresight *and* be on the watch to look [after one another], to see that no one falls back from *and* fails to secure God's grace (His unmerited favor and spiritual blessing), in order that no root of resentment (rancor, bitterness, or hatred) shoots forth and causes trouble *and* bitter torment, and the many become contaminated *and* defiled by it."

We are to live at peace with everyone, not for them alone, but also for us. If you have resentment in your heart, you are going to have major trouble in relationships—well, as the author of Hebrews put it, "bitter torment." From this resentment, many can be contaminated. Behaviors associated with resentment can include: negative attitudes, making life difficult, saying mean things, not wanting to spend time with a person who hurt you, putting the person down publically, or holding back on intimacy. I have seen people who lived resenting others and it ruined their life. They always felt like the victim and blamed everyone else for their problems.

I write this book with the utmost love for every person reading it. That is the reason I am being honest with you right now. Take a look at your heart and ask yourself, *Is Kristi referring to me?*

Are you currently carrying resentment because of your pain? I know for me, I had to keep my heart pure in this area. When my husband, Kraig, had to leave town because he was too stressed out, I began to resent him. I realized that he had left me to take care of everything and he got to leave town. Sometimes that thought would come into my head and I would begin to have problems. I would feel sick to my stomach, get a headache, and cry. I would then catch myself, ask God to forgive me for feeling the resentment, and peace would return.

Luke 23:34 states, "And Jesus prayed, Father, forgive them, for they know not what they do..." I think this is fitting here. I always say "hurting people hurt people." If you are hurt, chances are it is because whoever hurt you was hurting. Jesus knew the people had no idea what they were doing. However, you and I could argue they knew exactly what they were doing. On one hand, they did know they were killing a man named Jesus. But they had no idea the ramifications of those behaviors. I think it is the same when hurting people hurt people. They may know their behaviors are wrong but have no idea of the ramifications behind those behaviors.

Take this time to search your heart and ask God to search your heart also to see if you are holding on to any anger or resentment. They are not the same thing, either. Anger is more of an emotion, whereas resentment is more of a thought process and attitude. I *feel* angry as opposed to I *carry* resentment. Resentment develops when

anger is left hidden or not dealt with. Resentment goes to the core of our thought life and becomes an attitude of the heart.

I John 2:9-11 states, "Whoever says he is in the Light and [yet] hates his brother [Christian, born-again child of God his Father] is in darkness even until now. 10 Whoever loves his brother [believer] abides (lives) in the Light, and in It *or* in Him there is no occasion for stumbling *or* cause for error *or* sin. 11 But he who hates (detests, despises) his brother [in Christ] is in darkness and walking (living) in the dark; he is straying *and* does not perceive *or* know where he is going, because the darkness has blinded his eyes."

I have come across people who call themselves Christians but state they hate someone. People who do this are actually walking in darkness, according to John. It is so easy for people to become blinded to their own sins because their focus is solely on the sin of others.

During conferences where I have preached, people would want prayer at the altar for healing. Yet nothing would happen. I would ask them if they had any unforgiveness in their heart and most of the time the reply was yes. I would tell them if they really wanted healing, they would have to give up the unforgiveness. Many times, the people were healed once they gave that up.

PEACE THROUGH FORGIVENESS

I want to take forgiveness even deeper emotionally. Not only do we need to forgive so God can forgive us, so anger and resentment cannot get a foothold, but also so we can have peace.

I have often said that forgiving someone is for you, not them. When you hold on to unforgiveness, you allow that person to live rent-free in your head. Unforgiveness brings about headaches, stomachaches, stress, an increase in blood pressure, unheard prayers, a broken relationship with God, and also torment. When was the last time you truly had peace while still holding on to unforgiveness? NEVER!

I believe God wants us to forgive others so we can let go and let Him take care of the situation and us. Luke 1:76-79 states, "And you, little one, shall be called a prophet of the Most High; for you shall go on before the face of the Lord to make ready His ways, 77 To bring *and* give the knowledge of salvation to His people in the forgiveness *and*

remission of their sins. 78 Because of *and* through the heart of tender mercy *and* loving-kindness of our God, a Light from on high will dawn upon us *and* visit [us]. 79 To shine upon *and* give light to those who sit in darkness and in the shadow of death, to direct *and* guide our feet in a straight line into the way of peace."

The above scripture is referring to John the Baptist. This was his calling, to bring each person into the way of peace. I believe that is what this chapter is all about: taking you by the hand and leading you to the pathway of peace. It is called forgiveness.

The only way to have true peace is through forgiveness. II Peter I describes characteristics that each of us needs to develop: faith, virtue, knowledge, self-control, steadfastness, godliness, brotherly affection, and Christian love. However, Peter continues in II Peter 1:9 and states, "For whoever lacks these qualities is blind, [spiritually] shortsighted, seeing only what is near to him, and has become oblivious [to the fact] that he was cleansed from his old sins." We need to remember that we were forgiven. When unforgiveness is allowed, then godly characteristics cannot develop in us. When this happens, then peace cannot coincide.

Do you have a medical condition? If you do, ask God to search your heart for any areas of anger, resentment, and unforgiveness. This may be the reason you have not received your healing. I want you to know that this is not the case in every situation or the majority of situations. However, could it be your case? Remember that your prayers are hindered when you hold on to anger, resentment, and unforgiveness.

Luke 6:35-38 says, "But love your enemies and be kind *and* do good [doing favors so that someone derives benefit from them]...36 So be merciful (sympathetic, tender, responsive, and compassionate) even as your Father is [all these]. 37 Judge not [neither pronouncing judgment nor subjecting to censure], and you will not be judged; do not condemn *and* pronounce guilty, and you will not be condemned *and* pronounced guilty; acquit *and* forgive *and* release (give up resentment, let it drop), and you will be acquitted *and* forgiven *and* released. 38 Give, and [gifts] will be given to you; good measure, pressed down, shaken together, and running

over, will they pour into [the pouch formed by] the bosom [of your robe and used as a bag]. For with the measure you deal out [with the measure you use when you confer benefits on others], it will be measured back to you."

In one paragraph, the sum of this chapter occurs. What you do unto others will be dealt unto you. If you forgive, you will be forgiven. If you judge, you will be judged. If you condemn, you will be condemned. The measuring stick you use on others will be used on you.

If you forgive because you know that you are not perfect and have made mistakes, then when you make a mistake, others will forgive you. If you are merciful, your Father in heaven will be merciful to you. Peace can then flow like a river.

I want to repeat that I know this process is not easy. If it were, would there be so many scriptures in the Bible that discuss it? If you are stuck on this issue, spend extra time in your Bible reading every scripture on forgiveness. I went through that process and it was liberating. The scriptures I used were just a minority on forgiveness. Pick up a concordance, look up the word "forgiveness," and read every scripture on it. This will help you want to forgive even more. Mark 11:25-26, Ephesians 4:32, Romans 4:7-8, and Colossians 3:13 are other scriptures that address forgiveness.

Pray and ask God to help you want to forgive. If you know you want to forgive but are finding it a difficult process, pray. Ask God to help you let go of the anger, resentment, and bitterness. Ask God to help you give it all to Him. You will look back and begin to see how God can take away your anger, and your love for Him and peace will increase.

Once you have the desire to forgive, every time you have negative thoughts toward the person, remind yourself that individual is forgiven and pray and ask God to help heal those thoughts. Realize the enemy is going to keep bringing up the thoughts until he knows you are serious in actually forgiving. Keep taking the thoughts to God and speaking forgiveness. Carry the above scriptures around with you so when you begin to think about how angry you are, you can read them and pray to let the negative feelings go.

Forgiveness is a process. You have to actually process the harm done to you prior to forgiving the person. Being honest about the harm helps the forgiveness process. Also, you may need help processing the pain and moving toward forgiveness. I would encourage you to seek out your pastor, pastor's spouse, Christian counselor, or another mature Christian to help you if you are finding forgiveness difficult.

This chapter is not intended to be all-inclusive on forgiveness. It is a step to let you know the importance of forgiving and being healed from being broken. Allow God to help you forgive.

~ Chapter 13 ~
Battleground

I pray you are beginning to feel some life coming back into your situation. If not, keep going because it is about to happen. This chapter solely focuses on doing battle. By doing battle, I am referring to overcoming, working through, and dealing with your situation in a healthy way so you do not continue to feel overwhelmed. We know the battle is the Lord's, but He gives us ways to keep it in His hands instead of us trying to resolve it. In my own life, these are the ways I kept making it through each and every day until the Lord changed my circumstances.

Before I begin, I want to say something about God's suddenness. If you read through the Bible, you will see "suddenly" or "but God." These words are very important and are key words. These words mean that God has shown up. You need a "suddenly" or a "but God" right now. I know you do because I have been right where you are. This is a time when you will see a "suddenly" or a "but God." The battleground is the most important place.

James 4:7 states, "So be subject to God. Resist the devil [stand firm against him], and he will flee from you." Before you can be effective in battle you have to be subject to God. You have to be living right, turning to God, and being led by God. This does not mean you are perfect, but that you rely on God. The battleground is where you stand firm against the enemy. Yes, the battle is God's, but you need to stand firm. Keep pressing into God even if you do not see any changes. Keep your eyes on Him until deliverance comes.

Ephesians 6:11-13 states, "Put on God's whole armor [the armor of a heavy-armed soldier which God supplies], that you may be able successfully to stand up against [all] the strategies *and* the deceits of the devil. 12 For we are not wrestling with flesh and blood [contending only with physical opponents], but against the despotisms, against the pow-

er, against [the master spirits who are] the world rulers of this present darkness, against the spirit forces of wickedness in the heavenly (supernatural) sphere. 13 Therefore put on God's complete armor, that you may be able to resist and stand your ground on the evil day [of danger], and, having done all [the crisis demands], to stand [firmly in your place]."

This is one of my favorite passages in scripture. First, we are to put on armor that God gives us. We do not have to try to figure anything out, just follow God. This armor will help us to stand up against the devil.

Second, we do not wrestle with other people. This was a concept that I held on to tightly when I was going through my season of brokenness. I would have to remind myself that people are not my problem but that the devil works through people. There have been times that the devil worked through me and sometimes I was aware of it and other times I had no idea. This realization can help you not to become angry with people but at the devil, and fuel your fire to stand strong.

Lastly, the full armor has to be put on. All parts of the armor are important to be able to stand firmly in your place. I love how the *Amplified Bible* puts it: "Having done all the crisis demands, to stand firmly in your place." The crisis demands a lot from you and out of you. However, when you put on the armor of God, you WILL be able to stand firm!

Here is a list of activities that will help you stand firm and do all that the crisis demands. You will come out the victor:

PUT ON THE ARMOR OF GOD

The importance of the armor is mentioned above, but what actually is the armor? Ephesians 6:14-17 lists the different armor pieces. Verse 14 states, "Stand therefore [hold your ground], having tightened the belt of truth around your loins…" The belt of truth is the centerpiece of the armor. It is to go around your waist, the part of your body that stabilizes you and grounds you the most. You have to know the truth! This is the reason that I encouraged you to read the Word. How can you wear the belt of truth if you do not know what truth is?

The rest of verse 14 states, "…and having put on the breastplate of integrity *and* of moral rectitude *and* right standing with God." You have to have the right relationship with God to protect your heart. When looking at battle armor, the breastplate goes from the top of the chest and usually covered all the way down to the pelvic area. When you walk with the Lord and with integrity, then you protect your heart and all your vital organs.

Verse 15 states, "And having shod your feet in preparation [to face the enemy with firm-footed stability, the promptness, and the readiness produced by the good news] of the Gospel of peace." The important part of this piece of armor is to walk in the peace of God. The Gospel allows us to firmly plant our footing, just as the soldiers used to have nails on the bottom of their sandals when going to war so their feet would not slip. We do not have to walk in fear because we know peace.

Verse 16 states, "Lift up over all the [covering] shield of saving faith, upon which you can quench all the flaming missiles of the wicked [one]." The shield is our faith in God. This shield is very large and covers almost all of our body. It protects us from the devil hitting us. Faith is always out front of everything else.

Verse 17 states, "And take the helmet of salvation…" The helmet of salvation protects our mind and our thinking. Knowing who you are in Christ and knowing Him as Savior can keep your thoughts in line with the Word of God.

Verse 17 continues with "…and the sword that the Spirit wields, which is the Word of God." The sword is our only offensive armor piece. We are to speak God's Word over our life, body, situation, and mind. In the previous chapter, I addressed the importance of knowing the Word of God. It is important to read the Word so you know what to wield in the face of the devil.

PRAISE HIM!

Psalm 100:4 states, "Enter into His gates with thanksgiving *and* a thank offering and into His courts with praise! Be thankful *and* say so to Him, bless *and* affectionately praise His name!" Another great way to battle is to praise God. We come into His presence with praise.

I can remember when my heart was broken and I felt like crying, I would hear the still, small voice saying, "Praise Me." Putting on the praise music was very helpful. Even though I was unable to sing and could only cry at times, I would raise my hands and speak from my heart: "Lord you know these words are how I feel even though I cannot speak them because of my sobbing."

Before I knew it, the tears would dry up and the words would begin to come out of my mouth. My sadness would be turned into joy when the focus was completely on God. God alone can do that!

As I type this right now, tears come to my eyes in remembrance of how good God was to me in those dark times. With just ten minutes of praising and worshiping Him, I would forget about my problems and be totally focused on how big He is. This is the purpose of praise—to take the focus off of ourselves and our situations and place it on God. The presence of God will permeate the area where you are and the devil must flee when not invited to be there!

Praise can happen anywhere, anytime, and without music. Praise comes from knowing Who God really is. A helpful reminder is to begin with "A" in the alphabet and go all the way to "Z" with words that describe God. In your car, in the shower, at work—it does not matter where. The only aspect that does matter is that you do it!

LOVE OTHERS

John 13:34 states, "I give you a new commandment: that you should love one another. Just as I have loved you, so you too should love one another." Jesus commands us to love one another. When people are down, I encourage them to take cookies to a nursing home and spend time with the residents. Why? When you take your eyes off of your own circumstances and you reach out and love someone else, you receive a reward.

Romans 12:21 states, "Do not let yourself be overcome by evil, but overcome (master) evil with good." The quickest way to get ahead in battle is to love others. When the devil would rather you hide and stick your head in the sand, or, even worse, lash out and say or do something mean and spiteful, this is when you do something good for someone else.

Paul says "to master evil," not just to get by, but to master it. When you consistently live in love, then you are mastering evil. Watch how quickly your attitude will change and your view of your situation will alter.

SPEAK THE WORD

I have touched upon this a couple of times so far, but now I want to go into detail. The Word is alive and powerful; that I have already mentioned. But what makes the power go into effect? Speaking it!

Isaiah 55:11 states, "So shall My word be that goes forth out of My mouth: it shall not return to Me void [without producing any effect, useless], but it shall accomplish that which I please *and* purpose, and it shall prosper in the thing for which I sent it." I love this scripture. You can trust that the words you speak from the Bible will accomplish things! If you say you are more than a conqueror, then you will be because God's Word will accomplish what it says. Speak the Word every day, even multiple times a day, to bring life, light, and love into your situation.

Isaiah 65:16 says, "So [it shall be] that he who invokes a blessing on himself in the land shall do so by saying..." You invoke a blessing or a curse depending on what you say. When you speak the Word of God, you invoke a blessing. When you speak words of complaint, hardship, or negative confessions, then you invoke a curse. The choice is yours.

Proverbs 18:21 tells us, "Death and life are in the power of the tongue, and they who indulge in it shall eat the fruit of it [for death or life]." What you speak will bring death or life. Again, choose life.

I cannot stress the importance of this scripture. When you speak death over yourself, your situation will remain the same or worsen. Words that you speak, come over you. Yes, they are in your thoughts and in your mouth, but when you speak, those words then come over your life. You can become so focused on your problems that you will go deeper into depression and despair. Maybe you are there right now. If you are, begin to speak the Word and see the results that occur. You will begin to feel better and your situation will appear to improve just because you have chosen life-giving words.

Genesis 1:2-3 says, "The earth was without form and an empty waste, and darkness was upon the face of the very great deep. The Spirit of God was moving (hovering, brooding) over the face of the waters, 3 And God said, Let there be light; and there was light." *"God said…"* What are you saying? On the battleground, you need to be saying the Word of God.

Romans 4:17 states, "…Who gives life to the dead and speaks of the non-existent thing that [He has foretold and promised] as if they already existed." Your situation may not have changed yet, but speak like it has. "God is changing my circumstances. God has provided a way out. God has met my every need." Speak life! Are you saying, "God is a rewarder of those who seek Him"? Or are you saying, "My situation will never change"?

The battleground is a place for people who are serious about overcoming life's hardships. What you are speaking shows how serious you are about God and the trust you have in His Word. Write down your favorite scriptures right now and carry them with you. When you start to have negative thoughts, speak the Word of God against those thoughts. Oh, how God's Word strengthened me through the days.

THINK ON THESE THINGS

Philippians 4:8 states, "For the rest, brethren, whatever is true, whatever is worthy of reverence *and* is honorable *and* seemly, whatever is just, whatever is pure, whatever is lovely *and* lovable, whatever is kind *and* winsome *and* gracious, if there is any virtue *and* excellence, if there is anything worthy of praise, think on *and* weigh *and* take account of these things [fix your minds on them]."

I have heard Joyce Meyer say, "Where the mind goes, the man follows." This is so true. What you allow yourself to think about will become your reality. If you think on the faithfulness of God, then you will trust Him more. If you think about how horrible your life is, then you will make choices that intensify your situation for the worse.

One type of therapy I use when counseling is called cognitive therapy. This is when I help the person identify negative belief systems and distorted thought patterns and assist with reframing those beliefs and thoughts into a healthier way of thinking. That is what Paul is basi-

cally encouraging the people of Philippi to do: think on things that bring life and encouragement, not death and defeat.

One technique I utilize is called thought stopping. When you begin to have a negative thought, tell yourself, "Stop" and replace it with a positive thought. Continue doing this until it becomes a habit.

This is where knowing the Word of God comes into play. If you know what God promises you in the Bible, then you can think of those things—promises such as: God will never leave me; God will supply my every need; God loves me; and God is faithful. What are your thoughts right now?

PRAY WITHOUT CEASING

Ephesians 6:18 tells us, "Pray at all times (on every occasion, in every season) in the Spirit, with all [manner of] prayer and entreaty..." This verse is after Paul's discussion of putting on the armor of God. When the armor is on then you must pray without ceasing.

You can pray to God about EVERYTHING! Do not think anything is too small or trivial because to God everything about you is important. Some people stop praying when they know what they are doing is wrong. Do not stop praying. On the other hand, ask God to help you defeat the sins you struggle with. Do not become embarrassed or full of guilt when sinning, but go to God and ask Him to help you stop sinning.

Mark 11:24 states, "For this reason I am telling you, whatever you ask for in prayer, believe (trust and be confident) that it is granted to you, and you will [get it]." Believe that God hears your prayer and will answer you according to your faith and His will. You cannot pray to have a Mercedes so you can look cool and expect to receive that. But you can pray for God to deliver you and you know that is His Will, so He will answer you. When you believe God hears and answers your prayers, you will more likely pray about everything.

If you want more information on prayer, there are numerous books and scriptures that you can study. Prayer is not as difficult as some people make it out to be. Just cry out to God and talk to Him as you would a friend, straight from your heart, and you will not go wrong.

DON'T WALLOW IN YOUR TRIAL

James 1:3-4 states, "Be assured *and* understand that the trial *and* proving of your faith bring out endurance *and* steadfastness *and* patience. 4 But let endurance *and* steadfastness *and* patience have full play *and* do a thorough work, so that you may be [people] perfectly and fully developed [with no defects], lacking in nothing."

Allow your trial to bring you closer to God and to get rid of all unhealthy areas in your heart, attitude, and life. Then move forward. The more you complain and wallow in your trial, the longer you will be there.

One way to help decrease your wallowing is to distract your mind from thinking negatively. I encourage you to occupy your time with positive activities, hobbies, interests, or volunteering. When your mind is occupied, it is harder to wallow in your trial.

Remember, you bring blessings or curses upon yourself based on your words. When you wallow and complain, you bring about defeat and discouragement—not to mention that people will not want to be around you. Let me ask you a question: do people walk the other way when they see you coming? If so, chances are it is because you bring people down because *you are* down. Who wants to become a Christian when Christians walk around defeated?

Realize there is only one way out of your situation that will last and that is God's way. I do not want to sound harsh, but sometimes you need to hear that you need a better attitude and to move beyond yourself. The people I have found that wallow in their trials tend to be self-centered and want an excessive amount of sympathy or attention.

To balance this, there are times when crying is healthy and talking with others is necessary. However, I am referring to wallowing as those people who walk around and tell everyone everything that is going on. This is not in an effort to heal, but for attention. If this is you, ask God to help you stop. Ask God to show you how much He loves you so you do not need others' attention because you have His.

HAVE JOY

Nehemiah 8:10 reads, "Then [Ezra] told them, Go your way, eat the fat, drink the sweet drink, and send portions to him for whom

nothing is prepared; for this day is holy to our Lord. And be not grieved *and* depressed, for the joy of the Lord is your strength *and* stronghold."

Joy is not based on your circumstances but on your view. Is your view focused on your problems or on God's greatness? You can have joy in the midst of suffering if your view is looking to God to meet your every need.

In order to keep your joy, keep your eyes on God. The best ways to keep your joy are to praise God and read His Word. You can wake up every morning; make a decision and say, "This is the day that the Lord has made, I will rejoice and be glad in it" (Psalm 118:24). Or you can wake up and say, "Not another day!" The choice is yours.

LIVE BY WISDOM

James 1:5 states, "If any of you is deficient in wisdom, let him ask of the giving God [Who gives] to everyone liberally *and* ungrudgingly, without reproaching *or* faultfinding, and it will be given him." Do you need wisdom to make decisions?

Here is where I want to stress to live by wisdom and not your emotions. As a counselor, I encourage people to focus on what they know, not how they feel. Yes, it is important to recognize your feelings, but it is detrimental to be controlled by them.

You know that God loves you and that you are not alone. However, there are times you may feel all alone and want to go out to a bar to help decrease feeling that way. This is not only unhealthy mentally but dangerous spiritually. When you allow your emotions to control you, you are much more likely to make decisions you will regret later.

Proverbs 4:5-6 states, "Get skillful *and* godly Wisdom, get understanding (discernment, comprehension, and interpretation); do not forget and do not turn back from the words of my mouth. 6 Forsake not [Wisdom], and she will keep, defend, *and* protect you; love her, and she will guard you."

When you walk in wisdom, you are protected and defended. When you walk according to how you feel, you will have regret, guilt, more problems, and a longer time in the wilderness wandering around.

The best way to walk in wisdom is to take time to make decisions and to take time to respond when speaking. Take a day or two to make

important decisions and pray about them. When having to deal with a difficult situation, do not just speak but choose your words carefully.

You have to make a conscious choice to walk according to wisdom and not to how you are feeling in the moment. You cannot trust your emotions. You may feel scared, but the Lord did not give you a spirit of fear (II Timothy 1:7). You may feel all alone, but God says He will never leave you (Hebrews 13:6). You get the point.

GUARD YOUR HEART

Proverbs 4:23 tells us, "Keep *and* guard your heart with all vigilance *and* above all that you guard, for out of it flow the springs of life." This time of brokenness is when you are most vulnerable. That is why it is imperative to guard your heart.

Whatever is in your heart will rise to the surface. If you have anger in your heart, you will act out in anger. If you have jealousy in your heart, you will act out for attention. If you have resentment in your heart, you will act out of selfish ambition. From your heart springs your actions. You cannot hide what is in your heart because it affects what you think and how you act. People think they can hide things, but God sees and knows all. And, by the way, most people can also. Do not think you are hiding anything.

The Bible says do not let the sun go down on your anger otherwise the enemy can get a foothold (Ephesians 4:27). Do not let anger get a grip on you. Do not become jaded or cynical. Guard your heart from over generalizing about people or situations. Have you ever heard someone say, "They are all alike" or "They are all crooks"? Do not let anger get inside your heart.

Ask God to help you guard your heart. Ask Him to search your heart and identify any area that needs to be examined. Jeremiah 17:9-10 states, "The heart is deceitful above all things, and it is exceedingly perverse *and* corrupt and severely, mortally sick! Who can know it [perceive, understand, be acquainted with his own heart and mind]? 10 I the Lord search the mind, I try the heart…" Only the Lord really knows what is in your heart. Ask Him to search it and reveal to you any area that needs work.

KNOW THAT HE IS GOD

Psalm 46:10 states, "Let be *and* be still, and know (recognize and understand) that I am God. I will be exalted among the nations! I will be exalted in the earth!" In order to know that He is God, you have to be still.

Take time to be still in the presence of God. There is nothing like sitting outside or lying in bed and knowing that He is God. No music, no noise, no interruptions; just plain quietness and allowing the presence of God to minister to your heart.

If you are always moving around, always having to speak, or always having to have noise, how can God let you know He is near? How can you know He is God unless you take time to be still and just sit?

A friend of mine would ask me, "Kristi, does God need to Velcro you to a chair again?" If you do not take time to be still, God will give you opportunities to be still. Trust me, I would much rather learn on my own to be still than learn the hard way.

Those times of being still are now treasured times. I continue to this day to be still and I love just sitting and knowing that He is God. During my darkest hours, I would lie awake and God's presence would rest upon me. I would be so afraid to move because I did not want the warmth and love to stop. Once you experience knowing He is God, I hope you will never take it for granted.

KEEP YOUR PEACE

John 14:27 states, "Peace I leave with you; My [own] peace I now give *and* bequeath to you. Not as the world gives do I give to you. Do not let your hearts be troubled, neither let them be afraid. [Stop allowing yourselves to be agitated and disturbed; and do not permit yourselves to be fearful and intimidated and cowardly and unsettled.]"

Jesus gave you His peace. Stop allowing yourself to be agitated and disturbed. I really like that part. You have a choice. You can continue to allow things to bother you, or you can turn them over to God and allow Him to take care of it.

Psalm 34:14 states, "Depart from evil and do good; seek, inquire for, *and* crave peace and pursue (go after) it!" Not only have you already received peace, but you need to seek it, crave it, and go after it.

Only you can make this decision. Your pastor cannot give you peace. Your mother cannot give you peace. You alone have to pursue it and go after it.

What is keeping you from peace right now? I know for me in my brokenness, it was, *What if I never participate in ministry again? What if I lose everything again? What if I feel helpless again?* These questions would play over in my head until I decided peace was available and I did not have to ponder these questions because God was on my side.

Ask God to show you what is keeping you from peace. When God shows you, because I know He will, make a choice to give it to Him. God loves you so much that He wants you to come to Him and turn it over to Him. God did not give you a spirit of fear, and that is what steals your peace: worry, anxiety over what will or will not happen, when this will end, and how God will end it.

BE MINDFUL OF GOD'S MERCY AND GRACE

Know that God is a loving and forgiving God. Know that His grace can and will carry you through each and every day. Paul had prayed to God to take away the thorn in his flesh and God had said no. Here is the reasoning God gave. II Corinthians 12:9 states, "But He said to me, My grace (My favor and loving-kindness and mercy) is enough for you [sufficient against any danger and enables you to bear the trouble manfully]; for *My* strength *and* power are made perfect (fulfilled and completed) *and* show themselves most effective in [your] weakness. Therefore, I will all the more gladly glory in my weaknesses *and* infirmities, that the strength *and* power of Christ (the Messiah) may rest (yes, may pitch a tent over and dwell) upon me!"

What an awesome scripture. God is at His strongest when we are at our weakest. However, if you are not mindful of God, then how do you know God is at His strongest? The most important part is to be mindful. What does this mean? "Mindful" means to be aware of or to recall to mind.

How often are you being mindful of God's mercy and grace? Take time every day to realize that without His mercy, you would be lost; and without His grace, you could not make it through every day. God is always there for you, but you have to be aware of Him and recall Him.

The battle continues all around you. You know the battle is the Lord's, but you are on the battleground. You cannot escape the battleground, but you can escape defeat. Do all that you can and allow God to do the rest. Stand fast and see the deliverance of the Lord!

~ Chapter 14 ~
Take off Your Grave Cloths!

If you have gotten this far in the book, then I hope that means you are beginning to see light at the end of the tunnel. You may even be thinking, *I am on the upswing of being broken.* Once you have been broken, you then have to be restored. Restoration is also a process. During this time, you begin to process what has actually happened, what you have learned, and how to move forward.

This is not a time to hurry and move forward. I know that you are looking forward to moving ahead, but this is a critical time for you. If this time is rushed, you may not receive the full benefit of all the lessons learned.

> John 11:40-44 states, "Jesus said to her, Did I not tell you *and* promise you that if you would believe *and* rely on Me, you would see the glory of God? 41 So they took away the stone. And Jesus lifted up His eyes and said, Father, I thank you that You have heard Me. 42 Yes, I know You always hear *and* listen to Me, but I have said this on account of *and* for the benefit of the people standing around, so that they may believe that You did send Me [that You have made Me Your Messenger]. 43 When He had said this, He shouted with a loud voice, Lazarus, come out! 44 And out walked the man who had been dead, his hands and feet wrapped in burial cloths (linen strips), and with a [burial] napkin bound around his face. Jesus said to them, Free him of the burial wrappings and let him go."

This is the story of how Lazarus died and was raised from the dead. You may be feeling right now that you have been dead inside, dead emotionally, dead spiritually, but life has come. And in abundance!

I first want to point out that it took belief for Lazarus to be raised from the dead. Do you believe that God can bring new life to your life and situation? John 6:48 states, "I am the Bread of Life [that gives life—the Living Bread]." God can and does bring about new life.

Lazarus was called out. Lazarus could not give himself new life. He was completely dependent upon God. When God calls you forth from your brokenness, arise. Do not stay in your brokenness. God is beginning to call your name. Can you hear Him? Can you hear Him calling you and renewing your spirit with new life? It is imperative that you believe He is the giver of life. John 10:10 talks about how the thief tears down, but that Jesus gives life.

The most important part of the whole story of Lazarus for this book is how Jesus told people around him to free him. When Lazarus died, he was wrapped in burial cloths, cloths that kept him from smelling and decaying. However, when new life came, he had to take off the burial cloths.

This is a point that cannot be missed. So many times God begins to give new life to broken people, but they never take off the burial cloths. When the burial cloths remain on, the person cannot fully receive the new life. This is where most people get stuck. They begin to feel better and their situation begins to change, so they pull back from God because they are no longer so desperate for Him.

God did His part by bringing new life to Lazarus. Lazarus had to do his part by coming out of the tomb and having the grave cloths taken off. God can only do His part. You have to do yours. You have to take off the situation that broke you and all the feelings, thoughts, and emotions that went with it.

REMAIN IN BONDAGE

There are reasons it is so important to take off the grave cloths. First, when you keep the grave cloths on, you remain in bondage. Yes, Lazarus was able to walk out of the grave, but he was not able to move freely. When you have been broken, if you do not take off your grave cloths, you will not be able to move freely in the spirit or in life. You will always be in bondage to the situation that created the brokenness.

What do I mean? Had I not taken off the grave cloths of disappointment or the fear of failing again, I could never have moved forward. I would

have been too afraid to step out in ministry again. Who knows? This book may never have been written had I not taken off my grave cloths.

John 8:32 states, "And you will know the Truth, and the Truth will set you free." The truth is if you do not take off the grave cloths, then you will remain in bondage. Jesus is calling you to cast off your fears. He is calling you to cast off disappointment.

John 8:36 states, "So if the Son liberates you [makes you free men], then you are really *and* unquestionably free." When Lazarus came out of the tomb and the cloths were taken off, he was free, unquestionably and really free. You can be, too! Are you ready to take off your grave cloths so you will no longer be in bondage to the situation that caused your brokenness?

What would have happened if the people had not taken off Lazarus' grave cloths? He would have remained in bondage. The cloths were applied to him after death; however, they needed to be removed before He could live again.

Galatians 5:13 states, "For you, brethren, were [indeed] called to freedom…" You have been called to come out of the darkness and pain into the light. Are you coming? Galatians 5:1 states, "In [this] freedom Christ has made us free [and completely liberated us]; stand fast then, and do not be hampered *and* held ensnared *and* submit again to a yoke of slavery [which you have once put off]." Do not allow the situation to continue to hold you in bondage. Cast off the pain, emotional torment, and circumstances, and be free.

An important point here is to notice that people had to help Lazarus take off the grave cloths. If you need help, ask for it! Go to your pastor or pastor's spouse, counselor, or another trusted person to give you counsel or help. You do not have to do it all alone.

ABILITY TO SEE AND HEAR

There were also burial napkins over Lazarus' face. This impacted his ability to see and hear. When God gives new life, one of the most important aspects is being able to see the way forward and to notice where God is leading you. If Lazarus would not have removed the coverings, he would not have been able to see which way to go or hear what to do.

Psalm 119:105 states, "Your word is a lamp to my feet and a light to my path." If the coverings are still on, how can you see? How can you see the lit path when darkness still covers your face? Sometimes, brokenness causes us to become hard-hearted and bitter. When you refuse to let go of bitterness and soften your heart, you cannot see where God is leading you or even see Him at work.

Jeremiah 7:23 reads, "But this thing I did command them: Listen to *and* obey My voice, and I will be your God and you will be My people; and walk in the whole way that I command you, that it may be well with you." God is telling the Israelites to listen and obey His voice and walk in the way He commands. However, they did not listen and ended up back in bondage.

This is what happens when you do not take off the coverings from your face. You cannot hear what God says to you or see where He wants you to walk. This keeps you partly in death and partly in life. However, when any part remains dead, the whole thing lacks wisdom. This is when people begin to walk in their emotions or according to worldly ways because they are not seeing God move fast enough. So many times, God gets the blame when, in reality, it is the person who has never taken off the burial coverings so they are hindered from seeing or hearing God.

RESTRICTS MOVEMENT

The last aspect is when the burial cloths are not taken off the body; not only does the person remain in bondage, but it restricts their movement. Micah 6:8 says, "He has showed you, O man, what is good. And what does the Lord require of you but to do justly, and to love kindness *and* mercy, and to humble yourself *and* walk humbly with your God?"

How can a person walk when they are all tied up? I have seen mummies at the art museum and I cannot imagine how Lazarus actually walked out of the tomb. No one can walk, let alone humbly, when they are all tied up with emotions, regret, or resentment. God wants each one of us to walk humbly with Him, but being all tied up not only hinders the ability to walk, but hinders the ability to be humble. How can a person focus only on God when their movements are restricted?

We know Proverbs 31 refers to a woman of wisdom with all the wonderful characteristics that God has called us to. Verse 20 states,

"She opens her hand to the poor, yes, she reaches out her filled hands to the needy [whether in body, mind, or spirit]." When the grave cloths remain on, you cannot extend your hand to help anyone.

When a person goes through a time of brokenness, it can cause them to become very selfish and self-centered. This is what happens when the grave cloths are not taken off: "I have to protect myself. I have to take care of me. If I don't watch out for myself, no one else will." These are some statements that are made over and over.

How can you lend a helping hand or reach out to anyone else when you are so focused on yourself? You can't. You remain restricted in your movements. We often reap what we sow. Are you sowing helping hands or do you remain restricted by the grave cloths?

For me, if I did not cast off the fear of failure, I would not have been able to preach again. I would have been all caught up in what other people thought instead of allowing the Spirit of God to move through me. This would have kept me focused on myself, not reaching out to help others.

The importance of taking off the grave cloths has been addressed; I now want to focus on why people do not take them off. Here are the four main reasons: fear, it does not look like God has actually shown up, feeling stuck (just trying to survive instead of living), and self-pity.

FEAR

The most common reason people do not take off the grave cloths is because of fear: fear of failure, fear of disappointment, fear of other people, fear of being helpless, fear of success, fear of the other shoe dropping, fear of responsibility, fear of attention, and fear of leaving. All of these are different types of fear that cause people to remain in bondage.

Could you imagine if Lazarus would have said, "No, do not take off the grave cloths; I am too scared of what will happen next. I am too scared of dying again. I am too scared of what people will think. I am too scared of not making my life count." You get the point.

Have you ever heard of a self-fulfilling prophecy? This is when what you are afraid of actually happens. Why? Because you are thinking so much about it that you begin to act like it has already happened, therefore making people respond to you as if it HAS happened, which in turn, causes it to actually happen.

This is actually very biblical. Job 3:25 states, "For the thing which I greatly fear comes upon me, and that of which I am afraid befalls me." When you allow fear a place in your life, then negative things will happen. Sometimes people are afraid to step out again because of the pain they experienced by being broken. However, you will experience more grief and sadness because you will live with regrets. Take off the grave cloth of fear!

Psalm 55:5 states, "Fear and trembling have come upon me; horror *and* fright have overwhelmed me." Has part of your brokenness centered on fears? As a counselor, I try to inform people the more they try to avoid what they are afraid of, the stronger the fear will become. If you are afraid of driving your car, then the more you avoid it, the more stressed out you become if you even think about driving your car. The best way to deal with fears is to face them.

What happens when fears turn toward other people? Are you afraid of people? Proverbs 29:25 reads, "The fear of man brings a snare, but whoever leans on, trusts in, *and* puts his confidence in the Lord is safe *and* set on high."

This was one piece of grave cloth that I HAD to take off. I was afraid of how people viewed me since the church plant never got off the ground. I knew people were talking about it and would even make comments to me. If I continued to be afraid of what other people thought, I would never have been able to move on in my life. This specific issue needed to be removed and let go.

This is my prayer for you: Hebrews 2:15, "And also that He might deliver *and* completely set free all those who through the [haunting] fear of death were held in bondage throughout the whole course of their lives." Once God begins to bring new life, you have to take off the grave cloths of fear. If you do not, then you will remain in bondage in this area and will not be able to experience all of the new life that He has to offer.

There may be certain people who come to your mind right now that are in this category. You know God has delivered them and helped them to no longer be broken, but there is still something they cannot put their finger on that prevents them from fully living. Is this you? It is because God has brought new life, but the grave cloths have not been removed.

Romans 8:15 states, "For [the Spirit which] you have now received [is] not a spirit of slavery to put you once more in bondage to fear, but you have received the Spirit of adoption [the Spirit producing sonship] in [the bliss of] which we cry, Abba (Father)! Father!" God does not want you to remain in bondage. He wants you to cry out to Him and receive His help.

II Timothy 1:7 tells us, "For God did not give us a spirit of timidity (of cowardice, of craven and cringing and fawning fear), but [He has given us a spirit] of power and of love and of calm *and* well-balanced mind *and* discipline *and* self-control." How do you overcome your fears and take off the grave cloths? By realizing that God has given you everything you need to be able to walk in power.

God has given you love, wisdom, and a sound mind. Begin to use all of these things to allow peace to rest upon you. Say "no" to fear and "yes" to God! There really is no other way to face your fears than to do whatever it is you are afraid of in spite of the fear. Eventually what you are afraid of will no longer produce fear.

How did Jesus handle people who would try to make Him afraid? Mark 5:36 states, "*Overhearing* but ignoring what they said, Jesus said to the ruler of the synagogue, Do not be seized with alarm *and* struck with fear, only keep on believing." Who are you listening to? Are you listening to the God of all love or the father of all lies?

I John 4:18 states, "There is no fear in love [dread does not exist], but full-grown (complete, perfect) love turns fear out of doors *and* expels every trace of terror!..." God does not bring terror but peace. Keep trusting God and as you take off the grave cloths of fear, you will begin to sense His peace. This just might be the last issue that needs to happen before complete restoration!

HAS GOD SHOWN UP

Another reason people have not taken off their grave cloths is because it doesn't really look like God has shown up. You know your situation is better but it is still not over. Since it is not over, you are questioning if God really has delivered you. This creates an atmosphere of confusion and questioning.

Isaiah 43:19 assures us, "Behold, I am doing a new thing! Now it springs forth; do you not perceive *and* know it *and* will you not give heed to it? I will even make a way in the wilderness and rivers in the desert." Look to see where God has shown up. Sometimes when people are broken, they are so wrapped up in their brokenness that they cannot see anything else. However, God has shown up. Begin to look around you and perceive what God has done!

Perception is the main issue that impacts us. How you perceive someone or a situation will determine your attitude. If you perceive that God has shown up, then you will be more positive and hopeful. If you perceive that He has not shown up, then you will feel depressed, discouraged, disappointed, and hopeless.

Do you feel stronger? Do you feel more hopeful? Has something changed just a little bit? If you can answer "yes" to these questions, then God has arrived on the scene. Did the sun peek out of the clouds when you asked God to reveal His love? He is there and He has shown up. What has been accomplished in the spiritual realm will manifest in the physical realm.

I love the story of the walk to Emmaus with the two men and Jesus. Their eyes did not recognize Him, but their hearts were moved and burned within them while they talked with Him (Luke 24:32). How many times have you seen changes but did not give the credit to God? You or someone else became convinced it was a coincidence or "fate" that played the part?

Proverbs 3:5-6 states, "Lean on, trust in, *and* be confident in the Lord with all your heart *and* mind and do not rely on your own insight *or* understanding. 6 In all your ways know, recognize, *and* acknowledge Him, and He will direct *and* make straight *and* plain your paths." Just because you are having a difficult time understanding what is happening does not mean God has not already come to your rescue and delivered you.

I want to share this last story to help you understand that just because you do not understand something does not mean it is not of God. In Mark 8, Jesus is telling the disciples that He must suffer and die. Peter was not having any part of that! Here is Peter's response: Mark

8:32, "…And Peter took Him by the hand *and* led Him aside and then [facing Him] began to rebuke Him."

Can you believe Peter rebuked Jesus? It astonishes me when I read this story. However, don't we rebuke Jesus also when we refuse to see how He has taken care of us and the situation? When we are angry at God for not showing up, we tend to rebel or pull back. Isn't that rebuking Him? Have you stopped going to church or reading your Bible or praying daily because you think God has abandoned you?

Take off the grave cloths and realize that God has shown up or you would not be able to read this book right now. He has done SOMETHING for you in order for you to have picked up this book and purchased it or for someone else to have given it to you. Don't you think that is His way of answering your prayers? He has shown up—just believe!

Just because your situation does not look like what you thought it would doesn't mean that God has left you or forgotten about you. Romans 8:28 states, "We are assured *and* know that [God being a part-ner in their labor] all things work together *and* are [fitting into a plan] for good to *and* for those who love God and are called according to [His] design *and* purpose." God has come on the scene to work it out in your best interest and to further His purpose for your life.

BECOME STUCK

Another reason people do not take off their grave cloths is be-cause they become stuck. It is so easy to just focus on surviving instead of living. I can remember in my brokenness that God had shown up and things had begun to change. I was getting stronger in my faith again. My husband and I went away for one night and spend some time together. The next morning, I was lying out at the pool and began to feel tired again and just down.

I asked the Lord what was going on and here is what the Spirit spoke to my heart: "You are just trying to survive still instead of living again." It instantly resounded through my heart and mind. I had traded in living just to get through each day. The Lord wanted me to begin to experience life again.

Proverbs 5:23 states, "He will die for lack of discipline *and* instruc-tion, and in the greatness of his folly he will go astray *and* be lost." I

began to realize that I had no victory in my life and just existed. Do you know what I mean? Do you grasp what I am trying to say? There is a time to just make it through the day. The immediate crisis is the time to just survive. However, when the immediacy is over, then a different mindset has to take over. A mindset of "I am victorious" must arise or you will be stuck. When a person gets stuck in their brokenness, then slowly that person will be led astray to the world's way of coping. People begin using things such as alcohol, drugs, sex, pornography, and gambling as ways to deal with their pain and being stuck.

Have you ever said, "I just feel like I am existing"? If you have, then heed the Word of God. Hebrews 6:11-12 states, "But we do [strongly and earnestly] desire for each of you to show the same diligence *and* sincerity [all the way through] in realizing *and* enjoying the full assurance *and* development of [your] hope until the end. 12 In order that you may not grow disinterested *and* become [spiritual] sluggards, but imitators, behaving as do those who through faith (by their leaning of the entire personality on God in Christ in absolute trust and confidence in His power, wisdom, and goodness) and by practice of patient endurance *and* waiting are [now] inheriting the promises."

If you are feeling stuck, go to a trusted friend or pastor and allow them to help you become unstuck. You only get one life; begin to live it again. I know for me, when this was spoken to my heart, I began to live again. This brought about a renewed sense of hope, strength, and determination that I WAS going to make it through the loss and helpless feelings and the devil was going to be under my feet! I was NOT going to allow my brokenness to define my life for one more day.

SELF-PITY

The last reason people do not take off their grave cloths is because of self-pity. There are things that I am going to say in this part that may upset you, but realize it is because God loves you and wants you to have full life again.

Part of self-pity is the idea that "this is too hard." You may have gone through a lot and do not feel like continuing to push. However, when you begin to get wrapped up in this, it creates major bondage in your life. This is why you MUST take off your grave cloths.

Keep reading…Do you know that self-pity is actually pride? Pride is anything that sets itself up against God. When you are so focused on what has happened to you, then you are putting your situation or circumstances above God. I am saying this because the Lord revealed it to me first. Yes, it was hard to realize at first for myself also.

I was wrapped up in feeling overwhelmed by everything and kept repeating to myself and to God, "I am so busy. I have to take care of everything and I am overwhelmed. And ministry is too hard. I do not know if I want to continue in ministry or step out of it and go back to my own life."

One evening, I tried to tell my husband I was overly tired, burned out, and needed a vacation. This did not go so well, so I went upstairs to our bedroom and proceeded to tell God how unfair this was and everything that I had been through. The Lord led me to Proverbs 11:2, "When swelling *and* pride come, then emptiness *and* shame come also, but with the humble (those who are lowly, who have been pruned or chiseled by trial, and renounce self) are skillful *and* godly Wisdom *and* soundness."

I wish I could say my first response was repentance, but it was not. I was like, "What! God, you have got to be kidding me!" I had gone through everything and now I had to renounce myself and be humble and get off the pity pot! Yes. I began to realize that every time I began to feel sorry for myself, I would begin to feel empty and angry. However, when I would keep my focus on Him, there was peace and rest.

Admit it. You know of people who only see themselves as the victim and never the victor. Are you one of those people? Are you so wrapped up in what others have done to you that you place your self-pity over God? Can you only see what others have done to you but cannot see how you are also a sinner saved by grace?

You may be thinking right now, *Kristi, but you don't know what this person did to me.* You are right. I do not know. But do you want to live your life in bondage? Do you want to live your life focused on how you have been wronged and remain empty and angry? Or do you want to humble yourself before the Lord and allow Him to raise you up?

Romans 12:19 states, "Beloved, never avenge yourselves, but leave the way open for [God's] wrath; for it is written, Vengeance is Mine, I will repay (requite), says the Lord." When you humble yourself before the Lord, He will take care of you and your situation. God is a

God of justice; allow Him to take care of the person who has hurt you. God will do a much better job than you would.

Part of being a Christian is letting go and letting God be in charge of your life. I wish I could say that nothing bad happens to Christians, but that is a lie. We all have situations in our lives that cause great pain and turmoil. But you have to take off the grave cloths and not allow self-pity to overwhelm you.

I Corinthians 10:13 states, "For no temptation (no trial regarded as enticing to sin), [no matter how it comes or where it leads] has overtaken you *and* laid hold on you that is not common to man [that is, no temptation or trial has come to you that is beyond human resistance and that is not adjusted and adapted and belonging to human experience, and such as man can bear]..." Self-pity is not an experience that you alone are tempted with. Everyone goes through times when they feel sorry for themselves. Do NOT get caught up in this, though.

The rest of I Corinthians 10:13 states, "...But God is faithful [to His Word and to His compassionate nature], and He [can be trusted] not to let you be tempted *and* tried *and* assayed beyond your ability *and* strength of resistance *and* power to endure, but with the temptation He will [always] also provide the way out (the means of escape to a landing place), that you may be capable *and* strong *and* powerful to bear up under it patiently." God has you by the hand. Do not let self-pity drag you down or make you think your situation is too hard.

Lastly, Mark 8:34-35 states, "And Jesus called [to Him] the throng with His disciples and said to them, If anyone intends to come after Me, let him deny himself [forget, ignore, disown, and lose sight of himself and his own interests] and take up his cross, and [joining Me as a disciple and siding with My party] follow with Me [continually, cleaving steadfastly to Me]. 35 For whoever wants to save his [higher, spiritual, eternal] life, will lose it [the lower, natural, temporal life which is lived only on earth]; and whoever gives up his life [which is lived only on earth] for My sake and the Gospel's will save it [his higher, spiritual life in the eternal kingdom of God]."

The truth is we all have our crosses to bear. Yours may be a spouse leaving you while mine was something different. It does not lessen the pain, but there is hope. Hope only comes when you are willing to take off the grave cloths and allow full life to flow to you and through you again. This is part of the process of healing from brokenness.

When you give up your fears, being stuck, not understanding, and your self-pity then life comes back and you will be restored. You serve a good God, Who loves you very much. You have to continue in that belief and move forward. Are you ready to move forward? Are you ready for the next step? Are you ready to give up your ashes for beauty?

~ Chapter 15 ~
THE EXCHANGE

You have been going through so much emotional, spiritual, and mental anguish. Your faith has been tested, your emotions have been pushed to the limit, your mind has been on overload, yet here you still are. You are also stronger than you have ever been. You have a quiet strength that runs deep. You are more humble now than you have ever been. I want to encourage you to not lose this. You are more reflective with life in general but also about God. You have been still more than ever, yet your thoughts have also been as numerous as the stars.

Do you get the tension between how your relationship with God has gone deeper, but your life has been turned upside down? This is how God works when we are broken. When we are at our lowest point, He reaches down and grabs hold of us. Then He lifts us out of the deepest pit and places our feet on the Rock, and our foundation is on solid ground.

I can remember a time when I had gone to an AGLOW meeting in St. Louis, Missouri. I had spoken at a previous event and really liked meeting with other women, so I went back the next month. The lady speaking had the gift of prophecy and when she was done, she looked around the room at people. She gave a word of prophecy to someone and while that was happening, all of a sudden, I felt a rush of the Holy Spirit inside of me.

I knew something was about to happen. The lady then looked at me and began speaking a word of prophecy to me. I will never forget what she spoke to me. One thing she said was, "God has picked you up. Even when you did not think you could go on, God picked you up."

This is what is happening or has happened for you. God has picked you up, whether from off the floor or the pit, and you are being transformed. As you know, this is a process. You cannot stop here.

Ephesians 1:4-5 tells us, "Even as [in His love] He chose us [actually picked us out for Himself as His own] in Christ before the founda-

tion of the world, that we should be holy (consecrated and set apart for Him) and blameless in His sight, *even* above reproach, before Him in love. 5 For He foreordained us (destined us, planned in love for us) to be adopted (revealed) as His own children through Jesus Christ, in accordance with the purpose of His will [because it pleased Him and was His kind intent]—" God chose you for such a time as this. Keep pushing forward and you WILL see the glory of the Lord.

You are in the home stretch of transformation. You have made it this far; do not stop. There is one last step you must complete. It is called an exchange. You must give God your brokenness so He can give you His beauty.

GIVE GOD EVERYTHING

Isaiah 61:1-3 states, "The Spirit of the Lord God is upon me, because the Lord has anointed *and* qualified me to preach the Gospel *of* good tidings to the meek, the poor, *and* afflicted; He has sent me to bind up *and* heal the brokenhearted, to proclaim liberty to the [physical and spiritual] captives and the opening of the prison *and* eyes to those who are bound. 2 To proclaim the acceptable year of the Lord [the year of His favor] and the day of vengeance of our God, to comfort all who mourn, 3 To grant [consolation and joy] to those who mourn in Zion- to give them an ornament (a garland or diadem) of beauty instead of ashes, the oil of joy instead of mourning, the garment [expressive] of praise instead of a heavy, burdened, *and* failing spirit—that they may be called oaks of righteousness [lofty, strong, and magnificent, distinguished for uprightness, justice, and right standing with God], the planting of the Lord, that He may be glorified."

In order for you to be completely restored, you have to give God everything—all of your brokenness. He wants to exchange your brokenness for beauty. He wants to exchange your brokenness for the oil of joy. He wants to exchange your brokenness for a garment of praise.

It is tempting to quit right here. Your life is better and things are moving forward. But you cannot stop here! This phase is where your trial turns into a testimony and your mess into a ministry. Trust me; I have been right where you are.

I could have left ministry and stayed where I was, not worrying about stepping out in faith again or walking down the road of rejection again for the world to see. However, I traded in my ashes for beauty, my mourning for the oil of joy, and despair for a garment of praise.

God went on to say, "And they shall become oaks of righteousness, a planting of the Lord for the display of His splendor." This is what is happening right now in my life. God is being displayed and His splendor is magnificent. He is getting the glory and praise. He has made me beautiful because of my brokenness. This can happen for you also.

Jeremiah 29:11 states, "For I know the thoughts *and* plans that I have for you, says the Lord, thoughts *and* plans for welfare *and* peace and not for evil, to give you hope in your final outcome." God wants to do amazing things through you. I know right now it is hard to see what the future holds. You are just so thankful to have made it through the days, months, or even years that thinking ahead is exhausting.

Here is where I am going to encourage you to push one last time. It is like having a baby. You are going through labor. You are exhausted, you look a mess, and you have been gritting your teeth, holding on to the bedrails for support, probably yelling, and maybe even spitting (nice picture, isn't it?). However, the doctor says, "One more push. I can see the head. It will all be over with one more push."

That is what I am saying to you right now. PUSH! Push past this one last thing. Lay down your brokenness at the cross and walk away beautiful. This does not mean you never think about it again or that there will still not be consequences because of your situation, but these memories or issues will not bring great pain.

BEING MOLDED

Philippians 1:6 states, "And I am convinced *and* sure of this very thing, that He Who began a good work in you will continue until the day of Jesus Christ [right up to the time of His return], developing [that good work] *and* perfecting *and* bringing it to full completion in you."

Isn't it good to know that God does not leave us in our messes but will complete all things in us? I know this brought great comfort to me. God did not bring me out of my mess just to leave me the same. He brought me out to complete a work in me. He does the same with you.

Paul writes about the fruit of the Spirit in Galatians 5:22-23, "But the fruit of the [Holy] Spirit [the work which His presence within accomplishes] is love, joy (gladness), peace, patience (an even tempter, forbearance), kindness, goodness (benevolence), faithfulness, 23 Gentleness (meekness, humility), self-control (self-restraint, continence)…"

These are the aspects that His presence works in us throughout our life, but being broken causes them to be burned into our soul. You tend to have more love for God because you have experienced it at a greater level. Joy rises up within you because you know that your Redeemer lives. You have more peace because nothing comes close to the storm you just went through. You have more patience because you have learned how to wait on God. You have more kindness because you tend to look at what a person is experiencing in their life instead of just how they act. You exhibit more goodness because you know what it is like to hurt. You show more faithfulness because you know the faithful One and how important it was for others in your life to be faithful to you when you needed it. You become gentler with others because you know what it means to be gentle. Lastly, you exercise more self-control. Because you had no control, you have learned restraint.

This is where the beauty in brokenness begins to be seen. When you trade in your ashes, the fruit of the Spirit is what makes you become more beautiful to God and others. People will notice a difference in you that they have not seen previously. Your speech, behaviors, and commitments will change.

James 1:2-4 states, "Consider it wholly joyful, my brethren, whenever you are enveloped in or encounter trials of any sort or fall into various temptations. 3 Be assured and understand that the trial and proving of your faith bring out endurance and steadfastness and patience. 4 But let endurance and steadfastness and patience have full play and do a thorough work, so that you may be [people] perfectly and fully developed [with no defects], lacking in nothing."

When I first came across these scriptures years ago, I was a little taken aback. I was astonished how someone could say these words— of course, until I began to experience trials myself once I really began living for the Lord. These words are so true.

We get caught up in the moment and trust me, no one likes being in pain or uncomfortable, especially in today's society. Everyone wants their pain to stop immediately. However, I have learned that God sees our lives from birth to death. He knows what is coming ahead. He knows what we need even when we do not. I am thankful for this. God has prepared me by using trials to strengthen me.

I would not be where I am today had God not used trials to shape me, form me, and make me who I am. I would have run for the hills had God not prepared me along the way. That is how good God is. He will use your ashes to make you more beautiful to promote His kingdom. It is all about His plan, not yours.

Remember Jeremiah 29:11 earlier in the chapter? God is and has always been preparing you for something greater. You were born with a purpose and have been set on a journey since the day you were born. When you exchange your ashes to receive His beauty, you are just one step closer to fulfilling your destiny.

Romans 5:3-8 admonishes, "Moreover [let us also be full of joy now!] let us exult *and* triumph in our troubles *and* rejoice in our sufferings, knowing that pressure *and* affliction *and* hardship produce patient *and* unswerving endurance. 4 And endurance (fortitude) develops maturity of character (approved faith and tried integrity). And character [of this sort] produces [the habit of] joyful and confident hope of eternal salvation. 5 Such hope never disappoints *or* deludes *or* shames us, for God's love has been poured out in our hearts through the Holy Spirit Who has been given to us. 6 While we were yet in weakness [powerless to help ourselves], at the fitting time Christ died for (in behalf of) the ungodly. 7 Now it is an extraordinary thing for one to give his life even for an upright man, though perhaps for a noble *and* lovable *and* generous benefactor someone might

even dare to die. 8 But God shows *and* clearly proves His [own] love for us by the fact that while we were still sinners, Christ (the Messiah, the Anointed One) died for us."

My friend, no matter what you have gone through, God loves you! You have a reason to rejoice. It is called glory. Some day you will be living in His presence. The joy of that day is what gives you joy and hope today. When a time of suffering passes, the beauty that is unveiled is the joy and hope of knowing how awesome that day will be.

Your character has been molded, formed, and refined. That is why you exchange your ashes for beauty. Your ability to move beyond speaks volumes to those around you who have observed the whole process. You have not been perfect or done everything correctly. But isn't it good to know that Christ's death has already taken those mistakes away?

I am being led to encourage you to continue to push. Someone reading this right now is thinking that being a Christian is too hard or that life is too hard, and you just want to give up. Your thought is, *If it is going to be like this, then I do not want to be part of it.* You know what "it" is. It can be a marriage, ministry, or a job.

Philippians 3:13-14 states, "I do not consider, brethren, that I have captured *and* made it my own [yet]; but one thing I do [it is my one aspiration]: forgetting what lies behind and straining forward to what lies ahead, 14 I press on toward the goal to win the [supreme and heavenly] prize to which God in Christ Jesus is calling us upward." Push past the pain of remembering the failures—yours and others. Let go of the ashes so God can give you beauty. Exchange and press forward.

You may be thinking right now, *Okay, Kristi, but what does that look like? And how do I do that?* First of all, let me comment on what it looks like. If your spouse left you, it looks like being able to trust other men or women again and not shutting yourself off to other people. If you are in ministry, it means stepping out again when you are prompted by the Spirit. If you are suffering from a medical issue, it means still having joy and lifting the spirits of others who are around you. In my life, it meant spending quiet time with God again on a regular basis, waiting to hear

His leading, and when I felt His promptings, to step out and follow. It also meant trusting God to take care of the people I love and me not worrying about them.

DAVID

I want to take time to see what it looked like in King David. In I Samuel 16, Samuel was instructed to go anoint a new king because the Spirit of God had left Saul. I Samuel 16:7, 13 states, "But the Lord said to Samuel, Look not on his appearance or at the height of his stature, for I have rejected him. For the Lord sees not as man sees for man looks on the outward appearance, but the Lord looks on the heart. 13 Then Samuel took the horn of oil and anointed David in the midst of his brothers; and the Spirit of the Lord came mightily upon David from that day forward..."

What an awesome scene. David goes on to slay Goliath (I Samuel 17) and fights many battles and wins. Women are saying, "Saul has slain his thousands and David his ten thousands (I Samuel 18:7). You would think that David is on a roll and since God is with him, then nothing could stand in the way. Unfortunately, this is far from reality.

David ended up running for his life for many years. He hid out in caves and was not treated like a king. He survived off the land, not the palace food. King Saul hated him and would not allow David to become king.

This may resonate with you right now. Maybe you married the man or woman of your dreams and life was good. But something happened and now you feel like David. Your thought is, *This is not how this is supposed to be.* You were the perfect family with 2.5 kids, good jobs, and a white picket fence. Then cancer happened. Then the abuse began. Then an affair occurred. Then a child died. Whatever it was, something happened and it broke you.

"But God"! I love when I read that in the Bible. "But God" usually means that God has proven Himself faithful as always and just in time. II Samuel 2:4 states, "And the men of Judah came and there they anointed David king over the house of Judah." Even though it took years before this occurred, God was faithful. David reigned in Judah for seven years and six months.

Then, it gets even better. II Samuel 5:3-4 states, "So all the elders of Israel came to the king at Hebron, and King David made a covenant with them [there] before the Lord, and they anointed [him] king over Israel. 4 David was thirty years old when he began his forty-year reign."

Can you imagine being anointed king as a teenager and then not becoming king until you were thirty? Imagine the years that passed and how David could have given up. But he didn't.

Now comes the how part. How did David do it? He gave God his brokenness and God gave him beauty. Yes, it took time. However, it was all worth it. David went on to win many battles and have great success. Everyone liked King David and he was a great king.

But even beyond that is my favorite aspect. Acts 13:22 states, "... He raised up David to be their king; of him He bore witness and said, I have found David son of Jesse a man after My own heart, who will do all My will *and* carry out My program fully." David was a man after God's own heart.

How did David make the exchange? You can read all about it. Read many of the Psalms and you will see how David did it. He cried out to God. He leaned on God completely. He even complained to God. The point, he kept going to God and exchanging his ashes for God's beauty.

JOSEPH

I want to go through one more person in the Bible, Joseph. Here is a lad whom God was giving great and powerful dreams. Joseph was set up by God to be a powerful man. However, he had brothers who were jealous of him. Does this sound familiar at all to anyone? Has God chosen you for a work and someone else is jealous because God did not choose them?

Genesis 37 tells the whole story of how Joseph's brothers sold him into slavery. How do you think he felt? Do you think he probably thought, *Wait, this is not how this is supposed to be. Why is this happening?* Did you have those thoughts?

Genesis 39 then tells how Joseph was taken and made a slave. However, God was with him. Joseph was then promoted. But, once again, he was treated wrongly and sent to prison. I cannot imagine what or how Joseph felt.

Joseph was in prison for something he did not do. Yet God remained with him. Why? Because Joseph had a call on his life and God promises to never leave any one of His children. Joseph's life was foreordained before the beginning of the world and so was yours. Finally, Joseph gets out of prison and is made second in command of Egypt (Genesis 40 and 41).

Here is where the story really unfolds. Geneses 45 tells of how Joseph reveals himself to his brothers and this is what Joseph says in verses 5–8, "But now, do not be distressed *and* disheartened or vexed *and* angry with yourselves, because you sold me here, for God sent me ahead of you to preserve life. 6 For these two years the famine has been in the land, and there are still five years more in which there will be neither plowing nor harvest. 7 God sent me before you to preserve for you posterity *and* to continue a remnant on the earth, to save your lives by a great escape *and* save for you many survivors. 8 So now it was not you who sent me here, but God; and He has made me a father to Pharaoh and lord of all his house and ruler over all the land of Egypt."

That is what it looks like when Joseph exchanged his ashes for beauty. But how did he do it? He remained focused on God's plans for His life. He also forgave those who harmed him. He realized that God had never left him and he trusted God to promote him when it was His time.

This is for someone reading right now: God will promote you when it is His time. Do not be angry at people whom you think have stood in your way. God has called you and He will promote you. But it is in His timing. God could not promote Joseph until it was time to prepare for the draught. The way for you to lay down your ashes completely is to trust God, to know that He knows the exact way He will promote you. This is when you will become beautiful to others, when you can walk in the peace and trust of knowing God already has it all planned out.

Galatians 6:9 states, "And let us not lose heart *and* grow weary *and* faint in acting nobly *and* doing right, for in due time *and* at the appointed season we shall reap, if we do not loosen *and* relax our courage *and* faint." Keep pushing and pressing forward. You are almost there! You have a reward awaiting you and blessings in abundance if you just keep going.

The most beautiful aspect that comes out of being broken is the statement that Paul made about himself in Galatians 2:20, "I have been crucified with Christ [in Him I have shared His crucifixion]; it is no longer I who live, but Christ (the Messiah) lives in me; and the life I now live in the body I live by faith in (by adherence to and reliance on and complete trust in) the Son of God, Who loved me and gave Himself up for me."

May this become your statement! Read the next two lines aloud: "It is no longer I who live, but Christ in me. I will live in my body by faith in relying and trusting in God through Jesus who loves me and died for me." Keep repeating it until you believe it—not just in head knowledge, either. There is a difference between knowing something and believing it in your spirit.

Are you becoming more beautiful? Have you exchanged your ashes for His beauty? For some of you, this will be a process in itself. It will take crying out to God on a daily basis for a while for His help. But hang in there. Your beauty will come. For others, I can already see the gray of your life turning into a beautiful array of colored gemstones.

CONCLUSION

Psalm 126:5, "THEY WHO SOW IN TEARS SHALL REAP IN JOY AND SINGING."

~ Chapter 16 ~
Conclusion:
A Time of Refreshing

You have been reading for a while now and hopefully you have absorbed what you read. I pray that God has spoken to you through this book and you find yourself in a place of peace. Your circumstances may not have changed greatly yet, but you know it is just a matter of time before they do.

I pray you have learned a great deal about God but also about yourself. You are stronger than you would have ever thought you were. However, you realize it is not by your strength but by the grace of God that you have overcome and will continue to overcome.

As time continues and you move forward, remember where you came from. It is important for God to heal the pain, but even more important to leave the scar. This is so you will never forget God's goodness, provision, healing, grace, favor, love, and presence, especially when you needed Him most.

Your appreciation for God has grown so deep. You have rawness to your relationship with God that was not present before. I know. I have been there. Everything has a beginning and ending. The only thing that does not is God. He is forever! You can trust Him, count on Him, lean on Him, and cry out to Him.

Ecclesiastes 3:1-8 reminds us, "To everything there is a season, and a time for every matter or purpose under heaven: 2 A time to be born and a time to die, a time to plant and a time to pluck up what is planted, 3 A time to kill and a time to heal, a time to break down and a time to build up, 4 A time to weep and a time to laugh, a time to mourn and a time to dance, 5 A time to cast away stones and a time to gather

stone together, a time to embrace and a time to refrain from embracing, 6 A time to get and a time to lose, a time to keep and a time to cast away, 7 A time to rend and a time to sew, a time to keep silence and a time to speak, 8 A time to love and a time to hate, a time for war and a time for peace."

As you can see, there is a time for everything. The time for you to mourn and cry is coming to an end. It is time again to laugh, love, and build up. Your situation began, but it is also ending.

I am so thankful that we have a God Who understands. Aren't you? I am thankful that no pit is too deep and that His arm is not too short. God will continually pull us up and set our feet on the Rock.

I actually had a dream where I was with my husband and dog. A wolf was attacking my dog around the neck and I was crying and yelling for my husband to stop the attack. My husband looked at me and instructed me to go higher. I turned around and there was this stack of rocks. I began climbing them and could hear my husband encouraging me to keep climbing higher. The wolf quit attacking my dog, walked around the other side of the rocks, and said to me, "You think I can't come up there, don't you?" The wolf was not fooling me. I KNEW he couldn't.

I tell you this because the Lord often speaks to me in my dreams, and in this dream He was encouraging me to come up higher with Him. The Lord has given me the wisdom to understand most of my dreams. In this particular one, my husband represented Jesus, my dog was the church plant, and the wolf was the devil. The devil was attacking the church plant and the Lord was encouraging me to run to Him and obtain security and protection from the devil by going higher with Him. The devil knew he could not get to me if I was up on the shelter of the Rock. I love remembering this dream because the Lord was telling me that He is my Rock no matter what the devil tries to do to me.

It is my prayer that you have climbed the Rock and have gone higher throughout your journey. The view up on the Rock is better than down below. Hopefully you can see more spiritual things than earthly things. Keep your eyes fixed on the Rock.

Romans 8:18, 28-31 states, "[But what of that?] For I consider that the sufferings of this present time (this present life) are not worth being compared with the glory that is about to be revealed to us *and* in us *and* for us *and* conferred on us! 28 We are assured *and* know that [God being a partner in their labor] all things work together *and* are [fitting into a plan] for good to *and* for those who love God and are called according to [His] design *and* purpose. 29 For those whom He foreknew [of whom He was aware and loved beforehand], He also destined from the beginning [foreordaining them] to be molded into the image of His Son [and share inwardly His likeness], that He might become the firstborn among many brethren. 30 And those whom He thus foreordained, He also called; and those whom He called, he also justified (acquitted, made righteous, putting them into right standing with Himself). And those whom He justified, He also glorified [raising them to a heavenly dignity and condition or stated of being]. 31 What then shall we say to [all] this? If God is for us, who [can be] against us? [Who can be our foe, if God is on our side?]"

God is for you. He has always been for you. He has never been mad at you. I know some people think God is mad at them but He isn't! God can and will turn everything into a benefit for you. Just like God turned my trial into a book, He will turn your situation into a blessing. Somehow. Someway.

A time of refreshing is going to come or has already begun for you. I love what Acts 3:19 states, "So repent (change your mind and purpose); turn around *and* return [to God], that your sins may be erased (blotted out, wiped clean), that times of refreshing (of recovering from the effects of heat, of reviving with fresh air) may come from the presence of the Lord."

You have made it through the fire and are recovering from the effects of the heat. A fresh air is blowing in your direction, which provides for full breathing and the ability to move around. All of the fresh air is from God. You have fresh air to run, play, feel joy, laugh, and enjoy

your life again. You are recovering from the effects of your situation. God will give you new life, new strength, and possibly even a new direction.

I have received a new understanding through my journey from Paul's words in Philippians 4:12, "I know how to be abased *and* live humbly in straitened circumstances, and I know also how to enjoy plenty *and* live in abundance..." I have learned how to live when my life was crashing before me, but I also needed to learn how to live when the refreshing times began.

STATE OF TRANSITION

It is a transition period to learn how to live again and really enjoy life. Sometimes guilt can come up when things are going really well. Sometimes fear of what other people will think of the refreshing times come into play, especially if your behavior caused part of the brokenness. I had to learn how to live in this time and so will you.

It is strange at first when the refreshing times begin. There is almost a sense of trepidation. You may be unsure about how to act or what to do with yourself. My advice? Live! Enjoy the refreshing times. Jesus stated He came that we might have life, to the full, and until it overflows (John 10:10).

Take time to enjoy the fresh air. Take time to do activities with family and friends. Take time to do activities that make you smile and enjoy life. Do not feel guilty that you may not be spending as much time with God as you used to. Enjoying life is spending time with God, enjoying what He has provided and being thankful for it.

You do need to continue to read your Bible, pray, go to church, and spend quiet time with God. However, you may not need the multiple hours a day that you used to. This is okay. Do not beat yourself up about not being as "spiritual" as you used to be. You have a new appreciation for God and your smile is a reflection of the love that God revealed to you through your situation. God wants to bless you. Receive it!

You are going to feel good and your faith is renewed and strengthened. You are full of new possibilities and your horizon looks promising. God will fill you full of Him. This is so you can be used by Him to encourage others. You are full of Him so He can pour Himself out of you.

This is one reason it is so important to enjoy the refreshing times. They will not last forever. Remember that I said everything ends. When the Israelites made it to the Promised Land, they celebrated and praised the Lord. They enjoyed the refreshing air. However, the hard work came next—they had to conquer the Promised Land.

You are not filled with fresh air only for yourself. Yes, you can become renewed, refreshed, and reenergized. However, God is doing this so He can use you in His plan. Enjoying this phase is very important. Do not rush it. However, know that this process is called "life" and this time shall also end.

The journey you just went through or are still going through may not be the only time in your life that you will be broken. But now you know that you are truly never alone. This will give you confidence next time you face a trial. Hopefully, it can stop there and not break you completely. The more you trust God, lean on God, and cry out to God, the less likely you are to relive this process of being broken and rebuilt. I am not saying you will or can ever avoid being broken, but where your eyes are set can determine how far you go down the road of brokenness.

REACH OUT TO OTHERS

One lesson to learn during the refreshing times is to reach out to others. II Corinthians 1:3-4 states, "Blessed by the God and Father of our Lord Jesus Christ, the Father of sympathy (pity and mercy) and the God [Who is the Source] of every comfort (consolation and encouragement), 4 Who comforts (consoles and encourages) us in every trouble (calamity and affliction), so that we may also be able to comfort (console and encourage) those who are in any kind of trouble or distress, with the comfort (consolation and encouragement) with which we ourselves are comforted (consoled and encouraged) by God."

This is a time when you will continue to see God move in your life. The wisdom you have gained can now be shared with others. Your mess is now becoming your ministry. Your trial is now becoming your testimony. This is actually how so many people become involved in ministry.

During the refreshing times, people are so filled with God that rivers of living water flow from them. There is no dam to stop the flow of God, so people notice the peace, joy, and life that flows from them.

Have you ever wondered why you were spiritually drawn to another person? Well, you were drawn because deep calls out to deep. In other words, they have gone through also and may have words of encouragement to give you. You needed to hear what the Lord wanted to say through the other person.

Just like right now. As I am writing these words, I can sense the Spirit pulling someone in to heed the message. Someone reading this is feeling guilty for being in a time of refreshment. Maybe something you did caused your brokenness, and you do not feel you should receive this refreshment. I want to remind you that you allowed God to come into the situation and He restored you.

Take off the grave cloths of guilt and know this time is ordained by God. Remember, there is a time for everything. The time for correction is over and it is time for refreshing.

As I expressed earlier, there is a time for everything and everything has a beginning and an end. Someday the refreshing time will end, but allow the peace, love, joy, and faith to continue and remain strong. No matter what you face, you are never alone.

Do you have any lasting guilt? If so, take it to the Lord so refreshing times will abound. Remember, God has a plan for your life. He is not mad at you. He loves you more than anything and He wants to continue to pour Himself into your life. Receive! Just sit still and receive all that God has to give and offer you. Know that you are never alone. No, never! Sit still right now and ask God to shower you with His presence and whatever gifts you need.

Thank you for taking this journey with me and for allowing me to speak the Word of God into your situation. As you move forward, remember how beautiful you are and that there really is beauty in being broken.

APPENDIX A

SECTION ONE-
Acts 10:34

Chapter One-
Psalm 138:3

Chapter Five-
Matthew 23:37
Romans 8:28
II Corinthians 1:3-4
Isaiah 61:1
Psalm 91

SECTION TWO-
Zechariah 4:6

Chapter Six-
II Chronicles 20:3
II Chronicles 20:14-15, 17
II Chronicles 20:29-30
Romans 8:35-39
Psalm 50:15

Chapter Seven-
Acts 13:22
John 8:44
Romans 8:35-39
Ephesians 3:17-19, 5:2
Proverbs 8:17
Romans 5:5

John 15:9, 16:27
I John 4:7-8
Psalm 46:10
Hebrews 13:5-6
Matthew 11:28-30
Jeremiah 29:11
Psalm 126:1-3

Chapter Eight-
Acts 6:10
II Chronicles 20:15, 17, 18-29
Ephesians 6:11-13
John 10:10

Chapter Nine-
John 16:33
Philippians 2:6-8
Matthew 3:13-17; 4:1; 26
Hebrews 4:15-16; 2:18
I Corinthians 10:13
Romans 12:21
John 1:12
Romans 8:15-18
Philippians 4:19

Chapter Ten-
John 8:7
Romans 3:23
John 8:11

Romans 5:8
Luke 13:2-3
Psalm 103:9-12
Acts 13:38
Romans 8:1
Proverbs 10:25
John 8:14-15
Mark 5:36
II Samuel 12:7
John 1:1, 14

Chapter Eleven-
II Timothy 3:16
Hebrews 4:12
Psalm 119:50
Jeremiah 1:12
I Samuel 3:19
Hebrews 11:6
Romans 10:17
John 1:1, 14
Romans 4:23, 9-12; 12:2
Isaiah 62:6
John 14:26
Philippians 4:19
Isaiah 53:5
Romans 8:37
Psalm 34:4, 7
Proverbs 18:24
Philippians 4:6
II Timothy 1:7
James 1:5
John 14:27
Nahum 1:7
Psalm 91:1-2
Proverbs 3:5

John 3:30
Isaiah 49:15
Hebrews 13:5-6, 8

Chapter Twelve-
Romans 3:23
Matthew 6:12, 14-15; 18:21-22
Ephesians 4:26-27
Hebrews 12:14-15
Luke 23:34
I John 2:9-11
Luke 1:76-79
II Peter 1:9
Luke 6:35-38
Mark 11:25-26
Ephesians 4:32
Romans 4:7-8
Colossians 3:13

Chapter Thirteen-
James 4:7
Ephesians 6:11-13, 14-17
Psalm 100:4
John 13:34
Romans 12:21
Isaiah 55:11; 65:16
Proverbs 18:21
Genesis 1:2-3
Romans 4:17
Philippians 4:8
Ephesians 6:18
Mark 11:24
James 1:3-4
Nehemiah 8:10
Psalm 118:24

James 1:5
Proverbs 4:5-6
II Timothy 1:7
Hebrews 13:6
Proverbs 4:23
Ephesians 4:27
Jeremiah 17:9-10
Psalm 46:10
John 14:27
Psalm 34:14
II Corinthians 12:9

Chapter Fourteen-
John 11:40-44
John 6:48; 10:10
John 8:32, 36
Galatians 5:13; 5:1
Psalm 119:105
Jeremiah 7:23
Micah 6:8
Proverbs 31:20
Job 3:25
Psalm 55:5
Proverbs 29:25
Hebrews 2:15
Romans 8:15
II Timothy 1:7
Mark 5:36
I John 4:18
Isaiah 43:19
Luke 24:32
Proverbs 3:5-6
Mark 8:32
Romans 8:28
Proverbs 5:23
Hebrews 6:11-12

Proverbs 11:2
Romans 12:19
I Corinthians 10:13
Mark 8:34-35

Chapter Fifteen-
Ephesians 1:4-5
Isaiah 61:1-3
Jeremiah 29:11
Philippians 1:6
Galatians 5:22-23
James 1:2-4
Romans 5:3-8
Philippians 3:13-14
I Samuel 16:7, 13; 17; 18:7
II Samuel 2:4; 5:3-4
Acts 13:22
Genesis 37, 38, 40, 41
Genesis 45:5-8
Galatians 6:9; 2:20

Conclusion-
Psalm 126:5

Chapter Sixteen-
Ecclesiastes 3:1-8
Romans 8:18, 23-31
Acts 3:19
Philippians 4:12
John 10:10
II Corinthians 1:3-4

References

1)   Lemley, K.A. (2003) *Forgiveness: Moving from bondage to freedom* Godfrey: Living in the Light Ministries.

Letter from Kristi ~

God is so good isn't He? It is my heartfelt prayer that your life has been positively impacted by this book. I would love to hear how this book helped you move forward in your journey. Visit the ministry website at www. kristilemley.com and click on the contact us button and write how this book impacted you. For a deeper study, there is a workbook that goes along with this book. You can complete the workbook alone or in a small group study.

May God continue to bless you. May He make His face to shine upon you and give you His peace.

Many Blessings,
KRISTI